# Designing Learning

ASTD LEARNING SYSTEM

# Module 1

ASTD
PRESS

ASTD Press is an internationally renowned source of insightful and practical information on workplace learning and performance topics, including training basics, evaluation and return-on-investment (ROI), instructional systems development (ISD), e-learning, leadership, and career development.

Ordering information: Th *ASTD Learning System* and other books published by ASTD Press can be purchased by visiting our Website at store.astd.org or by calling 800.628.2783 or 703.683.8100.

Library of Congress Control Number: 2006920956

ISBN-10: 1-56286-439-4

ISBN-13: 978-1-56286-439-2

ASTD Press Staff
Director: Cat Russo
Manager, Acquisitions and Author Relations: Mark Morrow
Editorial Manager: Jacqueline Edlund-Braun
Deputy Editor: Jennifer Mitchell
Sr. Associate Editor: Tora Estep
Circulation Manager: Marnee Beck
Editorial Assistant: Maureen Soyars
Production Coordinator: Glenn Saltzman
Cover Design: Alizah Epstein

Composition by Stephen McDougal, Mechanicsville, Maryland, www.alphawebtech.net
Printed by Victor Graphics, Baltimore, Maryland, www.victorgraphics.com.

# Contents

# Introduction

In 2004, the American Society for Training and Development published the ASTD Competency Model, the most recent in a history of more than 20 years of creating competency models. These models were created to define standards of excellence for the profession of workplace learning and performance as it grows and to assimilate new thinking and practice. A competency model outlines the characteristics of excellent performance in a given job, thus providing professionals a roadmap to plan their career paths and development and achieve new levels of effectiveness and success.

The ASTD Competency Model covers the workplace learning and performance field, which encompasses a variety of jobs whose ultimate aim is to improve human performance. Although the aim is the same, the focus can range from individuals to whole organizations and the tools can vary from assessment, to training, to coaching, and beyond.

A model for this dynamic and complex profession must paint a picture of the current reality and point toward the future. Because the profession spans a range of expertise, the model must be broad enough to cover all learning and performance jobs, but not so broad that it can be applied to jobs outside of the profession. Furthermore, the model must define the profession within the context of its strategic contribution to organizational performance and balance contributions to financial performance with an obligation to the well-being of people. To address these requirements, the ASTD Competency Model identifies three layers of knowledge and skill: foundational competencies, areas of expertise, and roles. These components of the model are discussed in greater detail in the *ASTD Learning System User's Guide*.

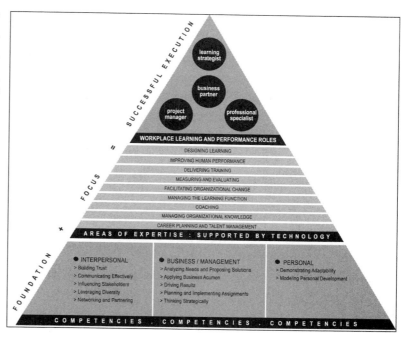

According to data collected to develop the ASTD Competency Model, designing learning, or as it is frequently called in the field, instructional design, is the area of expertise with the highest rating for importance and the highest percentage of time spent on the job. But why has this emphasis landed so squarely on designing learning? It has become a cliché to say that the world of work is facing far-reaching, rapid, and continuous change, but like many clichés, it is nonetheless true. In the face of such change, learning is increasingly critical to enable workers to adapt and organizations to sustain their competitive edge. Learning design is a key component in ensuring that learning supports organizations in their quest for excellence and meets the needs of individual learners.

The role of the learning designer is to design, create, and develop learning solutions to meet needs and to analyze and select the most appropriate strategy, methodologies, and technologies to maximize the learning experience and impact. How does the learning designer achieve these goals? To be proficient in designing learning, the practitioner must be able to combine the specific skills and knowledge enumerated in the area of expertise with an appropriate use of foundational competencies. Foundational competencies are grouped into three clusters in the ASTD Competency Model: interpersonal, business/management, and personal. In essence, these are skills that are relevant to all learning and performance professionals, no matter what their job title.

More specific to each area of expertise are key knowledge areas. The authors of the ASTD Competency Model defined sets of key knowledge that, when expanded, form the chapters of the *ASTD Learning System*. They comprise background information, procedures, tools, issues, best practices, and so forth that are necessary to be expert in any one area of expertise. For Designing Learning, cognition and adult learning theory, instructional design theory and process, and instructional methods are just some examples of knowledge that is regarded as critical to the practitioner's success.

Several of these key knowledge areas "crossover," or are related to other areas of expertise. In the case of Designing Learning, knowledge of various delivery options and media relates to the area of expertise, but is discussed in full in Module 2: *Delivering Training*. Conversely, cognition and adult learning theory is considered important for delivering training, but is addressed in full in this module, *Designing Learning*.

Closely related to key knowledge are key actions. Key actions are the behaviors and activities required for a learning designer to perform effectively in an area of expertise. Basically, they are what the learning professional does. One example of a key action is applying cognition and adult learning theory. This is evident when a learning practitioner designs a course that addresses the differences in how adults learn by ensuring that learners have some control over what they learn, including training techniques that connect topics with the previous experience of learners, ensuring learning is relevant, putting the learning into the context of real-life situations, and highlighting the value of the learning to learners. It can also be seen when a learning designer includes a variety of techniques to address different intake styles, for example, pictures and diagrams for visual learners, presentations for auditory learners, and games for hands-on learners.

Key actions lead to outputs. Outputs are essentially what the learning professional delivers. The table on the following page lists the key actions along with some examples of the outputs that arise from those actions.

| Key Actions (Do) | Examples of Outputs (Deliver) |
|---|---|
| • Applying cognition and adult learning theory<br>• Creating designs or specifications for instructional material<br>• Designing a curriculum or program<br>• Analyzing and selecting technologies | • Design specifications<br>• Learning objectives<br>• Content outlines |
| • Conducting a needs assessment | • Business case for learning solutions |
| • Collaborating with others<br>• Developing instructional materials<br>• Integrating technology options<br>• Managing others<br>• Managing and implementing projects | • Templates for instructional materials<br>• Learning objects<br>• Storyboards or scripts<br>• Job aids<br>• Instructor or facilitator materials |
| • Evaluating learning design | • Evaluation tools |

Creating outputs is what the learning designer does to get his or her job done and takes up most of his or her work day. However, the important point to remember about learning design is that it is undertaken in service of the big-picture goals of the organization and its people. Learning continues to be an essential competitive difference for organizations, enabling them to adapt to continuous change. Having the skills and knowledge related to designing learning is imperative for creating effective learning experiences for people that allow them to grow as individuals and contribute to the success of their organizations.

For more detailed information about the key actions and outputs, refer to the *ASTD Competency Study: Mapping the Future* (2004).*

*Bernthal, P.R., et al. (2004). ASTD Competency Study: Mapping the Future. Alexandria, VA: ASTD Press.

# 1
# Cognition and Adult Learning Theory

As Maresh (2000) points out, the next frontier in business evolution is the growth of the human capacity for generating and manifesting new ideas—and it is high time for traditional training methods to evolve as well. By understanding how adults really learn, learning how the brain functions at its peak, and applying this knowledge to instructional design, the workplace learning and performance (WLP) professional can create cost-effective programs that help accelerate learning and retention.

## Learning Objectives:

☑ Summarize the role adult learning theories play in the design of instruction.

☑ State the four theories of learning and instruction as defined in *The Trainer's Dictionary* (Reynolds 1993).

☑ Discuss Abraham Maslow's hierarchy of needs.

☑ Discuss Malcolm Knowles's concept of andragogy and its importance when designing learning for adult learners.

☑ Differentiate between adult learning theories and adult development theories.

☑ List the three types of learning as part of Bloom's taxonomy and describe one characteristic of each type.

☑ Explain the difference between teaching and facilitating learning.

☑ List Carl Rogers' guidelines for facilitating learning.

☑ Describe the individual characteristics of learning, including the roles that goals, experience, and culture play.

☑ Define the various theories of learning and memory, including cognitivism and behaviorism.

☑ Describe the concept of the learning brain model and how it relates to adult learning.

☑ Explain neurolinguistic programming and the three modes of learning.

☑ List six external and environmental influences that affect an adult's ability to learn.

☑ Explain Howard Gardner's concept of multiple intelligences.

# The Role of Adult Learning Theories in Designing Instruction

WLP professionals must understand the theories and concepts of adult learning needs and the reasons that some training techniques may work better than others. This chapter outlines various adult learning theories to consider when designing learning solutions. Practitioners must identify the characteristics and issues specific to adult learners to create effective instruction. Although trainers and designers often refer to a theory by the name of the individual who first proposed it, understanding a theory's relevance to adult learning is what is important.

The role adult learning theories plays in designing learning encompasses

- relating the design of materials to the differences in the way adults learn

- ensuring that learning solutions will reach learners

- explaining why training is designed as it is

- enabling WLP professionals to assess design to ensure that it meets the needs of learners

- helping to handle criticisms

- outlining how learning theory influences knowledge, acquisition, retention, and application of information.

# Four Theories of Learning and Instruction

As Maresh (2000) points out with regard to adult learning: "An understanding of how the adult brain learns is very important, but it is not the be-all and end-all. Applying that understanding to training design and delivery is the goal."

Although there are many theories of cognition and adult learning presented in this chapter, there are four primary theories of learning and instruction as defined in *The Trainer's Dictionary: HRD Terms, Acronyms, Initials, and Abbreviations* (Reynolds 1993):

- **Subject-centered:** A pedagogy-based instructional approach. Subject-centered instruction focuses on what will be taught as opposed to learner-related characteristics. Subject-centered instruction focuses on acquisition of information.

- **Objective-centered:** A behaviorism-based theory of instruction that concentrates on observable and measurable outcomes.

- **Experience-centered:** A cognitivism-based theory of instruction focused on the learner's experience during instruction and production of fresh insights.

- **Opportunity-centered:** A developmentalism-based theory of instruction that focuses on matching individual needs to appropriate instructional experiences. Opportunity-centered instruction is particularly useful for helping employees adapt to changes in their work lives.

# Abraham Maslow's Hierarchy of Needs

Motivating people to achieve their potential is one of the challenges in learning and performance improvement. To explain the foundations of motivation, Abraham Maslow introduced his hierarchy of needs in *Motivation and Personality*, published in 1954. Maslow contended that people have complex needs that they strive to fulfill and that over time, their needs change and evolve.

Maslow (1954) categorized these needs into a logical hierarchy from physical to psychological (illustrated in Figure 1-1):

- *Physiological:* These needs include food, drink, sex, and sleep.
- *Safety:* These include freedom from fear and the need to be safe and stable.
- *Belongingness:* This category concerns the need for friends and family.
- *Esteem:* This includes both self-esteem and the need to be highly regarded by others.
- *Self-actualization:* This is the need to be "all that you can be."

## Figure 1-1. Maslow's Hierarchy of Needs

Maslow contended that a person can achieve the next higher level of the hierarchy only after lower-level needs have been satisfied. This means that employees and learners are motivated by a variety of factors—and that those factors may be unknown or difficult to discern.

Most jobs satisfy needs in the four lower levels of the hierarchy: wages or salaries to provide for physiological needs, a safe working environment, camaraderie for belongingness needs, and the respect of co-workers and peers for esteem. Needs related to self-actualization link to the number and types of opportunities for

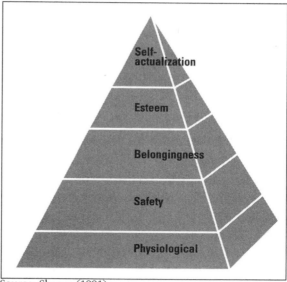

Source: Sharpe (1991).

growth and achievement the work provides. For WLP professionals, understanding learner motivation and factors influencing motivation is one piece of the designing learning puzzle. Establishing an appropriate climate and a sense of safety in a learning environment will help to satisfy the lower-level needs of adult learners.

# Malcolm Knowles's Adult Learning, or Andragogy

Malcolm Knowles, a leader in the field of adult education, was one of the first researchers to propose that adults learn differently than children. In his seminal book, Knowles

(1984) is credited with popularizing the terms **andragogy** and **pedagogy**. To understand the differences between pedagogy and andragogy, a brief introduction to pedagogy may be useful.

## Pedagogy

As Elaine Biech, author of *Training for Dummies* (2005), points out, pedagogy is a traditional style of teaching based on a didactic model, or lecturing. Generally, this model is content-centered and instructor-led. Pedagogy literally means the art of teaching children.

Whereas adults learn primarily because they want or need to, children's formal learning is usually led by someone else and is based on children learning specific tasks to prepare them to learn additional, more complicated tasks.

For example, children first learn to count so that they can later learn to add and subtract; then later learn to multiply and divide; and then later learn algebra, geometry, and so on.

Most people have experienced a pedagogical model of learning in which

- the instructor is the expert because the learner has little experience, and the instructor is expected to impart wisdom

- the instructor is responsible for all aspects of the learning process, including what, how, and when the learners learn

- learning is content-centered, meaning that objectives establish goals and a logical sequence of material is presented to the learners

- motivation is external, and learners learn because they must reach the next level of understanding to pass a test, or to acquire certification.

## Andragogy

Malcolm Knowles's theory on adult learning, also known as andragogy, contends that five key principles affect the way adults learn. These five principles are

- **Self-concept of the learner:** As people mature, they develop a psychological need for self-direction. They often resent situations in which they feel someone else's will is being imposed upon them. Adult learners learn best when they have a measure of control over their learning experience.

- **Prior experience of the learner:** As people mature, they accumulate experience and knowledge that become a resource for learning. Whenever possible, linking new material to a learner's existing knowledge is important for creating a powerful and relevant learning experience. In some situations, adults may learn new information that contradicts their current understanding and beliefs. In some cases, helping learners change their beliefs to accept the new information is critical. When possible, allow adult learners to assess their current knowledge and skip to information that is new and relevant.

- **_Readiness to learn:_** As people mature, their readiness to learn relates increasingly to their need to learn to fulfill their roles effectively. As Knowles points out, "Adults are motivated to learn as they experience needs and interests that learning will satisfy; therefore, these are the appropriate starting points for organizing adult learning activities." Adults participate in learning programs to achieve a particular goal and are most ready to learn information or developmental tasks when they can immediately apply the new knowledge or skills to real-life situations.

- **_Orientation to learning:_** As people mature, they seek knowledge they can use immediately, resulting in a shift of learning from a subject focus to a problem focus. According to Knowles, "Adults' orientation to learning is life-centered; therefore, the appropriate units for organizing adult learning are life situations, not subjects." Adults are motivated to learn to the extent that they perceive that learning will help them perform tasks or is relevant in dealing with real-life situations. They learn new knowledge, understanding, skills, values, and attitudes most effectively when presented in the context of real-life or experience-oriented learning situations.

- **_Motivation to learn:_** As people mature, their motivation to learn becomes increasingly internal. When challenged with a new job role or process, adults are motivated to learn. When adults become familiar with job roles and processes, fear or failure of having to unlearn something often decreases the motivation to learn. Only when a specific need arises that has intrinsic value or personal payoff is an adult motivated to learn.

Table 1-1 presents the most important points about the differences between child and adult learning derived from Knowles and other learning theorists.

## Table 1-1. Characteristics of Pedagogical and Andragogical

| Learner Characteristic | Pedagogical | Andragogical |
|---|---|---|
| Self-concept for the learner | Is dependent | Is self-directed |
| Prior experience of the learner | Does not use experience | Uses experience as a resource for self and others |
| Readiness to learn | Is directly related to age level and curriculum | Is developed from life experience |
| Orientation to learning | Is self-centered | Is task- or problem-centered |
| Motivation to learn | Is based on external rewards and punishments | Is based on internal incentives and curiosity |

# Adult Development Theories

That children change as they age is well understood and anticipated; however, regarding adult learning, it is only within the last few decades that it has become equally clear that adults also change as they age. As described by Sharan B. Merriam and Rosemary S. Caffarella (1991), "What has become problematic is separating facts, ideas, and theories about adult development from the popularized and fictionalized versions of research findings and then linking those findings to learning in adulthood."

Merriam and Caffarella discuss developmental characteristics of adults from three major perspectives: physical, psychological, and sociocultural with a focus on how the broad themes of learning and development are intertwined.

## Physical Changes

Although life expectancy has nearly doubled, longer life does not mean that the effects of aging and physical changes to vision and hearing are halted. As noted by Merriam and Caffarella, while adults age physically, the effect of these changes on the capacity to learn is still largely unknown. Three physical changes that have been shown to affect learning in adulthood include changes to senses (seeing and hearing), changes in the central nervous system, and changes as a result of major disease processes. Some training considerations include:

- **Sight:** Changes in vision can create problems with the learning process, for example, in the ability to perceive small detail such as words on a printed page or computer screen.

- **Sound:** Although changes in vision happen primarily at set periods in life, hearing loss is the inability of older adults to understand the spoken word. During training, this lack of hearing the information fully may mean that pieces of the information are lost so that the meaning may be altered for the learner.

- **Central nervous system:** The central nervous system consists of the brain and the spinal cord and forms the primary biological basis for learning. Although only limited knowledge exists about how changes in this system affect learning in healthy adults as they age, the most consistent finding related to changes has to do with a decline in reaction time, for example, to complete a psychomotor task.

- **Disease processes:** Although health impairments may affect the learning process, both cardiovascular disease and Alzheimer's disease have direct effects on adult learning, including loss of memory, difficulty in speech, and loss of mobility as a result of a stroke or loss of blood supply to the brain, impaired memory and disorganization of thoughts, as well as changes in judgment and emotion.

  Indirect effects of these diseases may include pain and fatigue, leaving participants with little energy or motivation to engage in learning activities; medications and treatments that may affect the way people think and behave; and financial drain on resources.

## Psychological Changes

According to Merriam and Caffarella (1991), the psychological perspective focuses on how adults develop over their life span. This framework focuses on how development occurs within the individual and in interaction with the environment as it relates to intellectual, cognitive, and personal development.

Although a number of adult educators have proposed useful ideas, from Merriam and Caffarella's perspective, Daloz's (1986) work best fits their stance. Daloz suggests using development theories as alternative maps of how adults can develop—without specifying which paths should be taken. Merriam and Caffarella indicate that this is the best approach by suggesting that there is no right or best way that adults develop as they age. Merriam and Caffarella note that with this approach, three concepts from personal development literature provide value in gaining a clear picture of adulthood: sequential patterns of development, life events, and transitions (Merriam 1984).

- *Sequential patterns of development:* This is the view that development occurs as a series of stages that adults pass through as they age. Often these periods are related to chronological time—either specific age periods or broad age parameters (young, middle-age, older adulthood).

- *Life events:* An alternative in which (Hultsch and Plemons 1979; Brim and Ryff 1980) "life events are benchmarks in the human lifecycle," markers that give "shape and direction to the various aspects of a person's life." As Merriam and Caffarella point out, there are two basic types of life events: individual and cultural (Hultsch and Plemons 1979). Individual life events, such as birth, marriage, and divorce, define a specific person's life. Societal and historical happenings—for example, wars, natural catastrophes, and the women's movement—shape the context in which a person develops.

  Knox (1977) and Brookfield (1987), among others, propose that engaging in learning activities is one way in which adults cope with life activities. According to Knox, "When a change event occurs, the need for some adaptation produces, for some adults at least, a heightened readiness to engage in educative activity."

- *Transitions:* Used by developmentalists who speak in terms of life stages and those who support the life events paradigm, transitions are viewed as "the natural process of disorientation and reorientation that marks the turning points of the path of growth . . . involving periodic accelerations and transformations" (Bridges 1980). Merriam and Caffarella point out that adults continually experience transitions, whether anticipated or unanticipated, and react to them depending on the type of transition, the context in which it occurs, and its effect on their lives. Many educators have linked the concept of transitions to learning in adulthood. Aslanian and Brickell (1980) found that as adults reassess their lives, they come to "the realization that they will have to learn something new if they are going to make the transition successfully."

## Sociocultural Changes

Merriam and Caffarella (1991) point out that understanding how social and cultural factors influence development in adulthood is gaining more recognition. The investigation of social roles has been a major focus of the sociological perspective, which views change as a product of lifelong socialization experiences (Brim 1968). A social role is defined as both a position and its association with expectations determined primarily by normative beliefs held by society (Whitbourne and Weinstock 1979). Examples of these various positions include parent, spouse, worker, child, and friend. Changes in social position result from modification of these roles—for example, from paid worker to retired employee. These changes may be initiated voluntarily or by others.

Merriam and Caffarella continue that additional research from the sociological perspective, exemplified by the work of Neugarten and colleagues (Neugarten 1973, 1976; Neugarten and Datan 1979) suggesting that theory should be built around the expected timing of life events in adulthood. Merriam (1984) summarized this work: "Within every social system, expectations develop as to the appropriate times certain events should occur. Each person becomes aware of the 'social clock' that suggests the best time to leave home, to marry, retire, and so on . . . ." Neugarten points out that the events themselves do not precipitate change—rather the timing—especially if they occur outside of the "normal, expected life cycle." When these events occur outside the normal cycle they are more likely to cause conflict and trauma. From this vantage point, the study of adult development focuses on the timing of life events rather than on the events themselves.

According to Merriam and Caffarella, the most comprehensive integration of the sociocultural framework of development into research and theory related to adult learning has come from Jarvis (1987). Jarvis contends "that learning is not just a psychological process that happens in splendid isolation from the world in which the learner lives, but is intimately related to that world and affected by it." Jarvis makes two assumptions:

- Most people take on the knowledge, values, beliefs, and attitudes of the society in which they live.

- A person is "a reflection of the sum total of experiences that the individual has in society."

Jarvis proposes an adult learning model primarily based on the experiences of the learner and outlined three possible classes of how adults respond to experiences, including nonlearning responses, nonreflective learning, and reflective learning.

As Merriam and Caffarella point out, adult development theory and research offer a rich array of material from which numerous implications can be drawn about learning in adulthood. The various perspectives presented—developmental characteristics, psychological changes, and social and cultural factors—are meant to provide a broad perspective about adult learners, the changes they go through, and how these changes motivate and interact with learning to structure learning experiences that both respond to and stimulate development.

## Three Types of Learning and Bloom's Taxonomy

As noted by Biech (2005), trainers often use knowledge, skills, and attitudes—also known as KSAs—to describe three types of learning. These three categories are the work of Benjamin Bloom and are part of Bloom's taxonomy, a hierarchy that organizes cognitive, psychomotor, and affective outcomes starting from the simplest behavior and ranging to the most complex: knowledge, comprehension, application, analysis, synthesis, and evaluation.

These three categories describe the ultimate goal of the training process—what learners hopefully acquire as the result of training:

- *Knowledge* (also known as cognitive) involves the development of intellectual skills. Examples of knowledge include understanding the principles of engineering, how to organize plants in a garden, or knowing how to complete a series of steps to complete a task or process.

- *Skills* (also known as psychomotor) refer to physical movement, coordination, and the use of motor skills to accomplish a task. An example of skills is the ability to operate a piece of equipment.

- *Attitude* (also known as affective) refers to how people deal with things emotionally, such as feelings, motivation, and enthusiasm. Although attitude is not taught, training may affect it. Although trainers can not change attitudes, they can often influence them.

Depending on the category of learning, instructional designers may need to use different techniques and presentation methods to help convey the content being taught. For example, methods that are appropriate for developing knowledge may not be effective for developing skills.

## Differences Between Teaching and Facilitating Learning

A key distinction exists between teaching and facilitating learning. Traditional education uses instructive-style learning sessions or lectures to teach participants. The instructor is the "teller" of information.

Facilitating learning gets participants involved and helps adults assume responsibility for their own learning. Facilitative methods obtain a high level of participation among learners and often leverage questioning techniques, solicitation of ideas, brainstorming, and small-group discussions to involve participants in the learning process.

Effective adult learning programs leverage both instructional and facilitative techniques to build new awareness, knowledge, skills, or attitudes and provide adult learners with the ability to apply the new information to real-life situations.

## Guidelines for Facilitating Learning

Traditionally, training professionals led instructive-style learning sessions. Many now believe that the facilitative or participatory training style—in which the trainer guides the learner to discover what he or she needs to learn—is more appropriate for adult learners. This trainer-facilitated and learner-centered environment better suits the adult learning styles.

Carl Rogers, a clinical psychologist, developed several guidelines for facilitating learning by starting with a viewpoint that, in a general way, therapy is a learning process. He proposed several theories of personality and behavior and applied them to education. This process led him to the concept of learner-centered teaching. One of Rogers' hypotheses, as noted by Knowles (1984), "We cannot teach another person directly; we can only facilitate his learning."

These eight guidelines, a result of Carl Rogers's work, help to facilitate learning. Effective facilitators

- establish the initial mood or climate of the group or class experience
- clarify the purpose of learning for each individual in the class as well as the more general purposes of the group
- rely on the desire of each learner to implement purposes with meaning for the individual learner as the motivational force behind significant learning
- organize the widest possible range of resources for the learner
- act as a flexible resource to be used by the group
- accept both the intellectual content and the emotional attitudes to provide the appropriate degree of emphasis to the individual or group
- act as participant learners
- accept their own limitations.

## Individual Characteristics of Learning

A key question of interest to andragogists and pedagogists alike is why people learn. Research suggests that adults learn only when they need to learn, no matter what the trainer does or how good the presentation is. When designing learning, WLP professionals must consider four key characteristics of learning: motivation, goals, experience, and culture.

## Motivation

Many instructional programs are designed to introduce the "What's in it for me?" (WIIFM) concept to orient learners to the key benefits of the program and to help motivate them to learn. The WIIFM mentality helps learners translate the external need into an internal need, even if that need is only to get training over with and to pass a test. This motivator is exemplified by the student who really has no internal need to learn algebra but internalizes the need as a need to graduate. Without this change from an externally motivated need to an internal one, learners will not learn.

Most often, the need to learn is some combination of internal and external needs. For example, a learner may have an internal motivation to learn supervisory skills because he or she has been given a new job title. The concept of team building, however, may be a subject that holds little personal interest. Yet, the external driver (the fact that this is part of the supervisory program) ensures that this part of the training program is completed.

In learning, if people achieve an objective—master a piece of information—and are rewarded for their success, the likelihood of retaining the learning increases. Recognized success for most people encourages them to learn and retain. When behaviorism was in its heyday, from the mid-1950s to the mid-1970s, the value and effect of reward was almost a sacred law. Cognitive research tends to temper some of the extreme enthusiasm for the power of reward, but almost all learning researchers still acknowledge the value of reinforcement.

There is a major distinction between intrinsic rewards, which emerge from the sense of accomplishment a person gets after learning something, and extrinsic rewards, which are associated with something tangible that a person is given for learning (for example, a gold star, food, money, removal of something unpleasant). The more trainers can include and build in intrinsic rewards, the joy that springs from the learning itself, the better it is for the learner. With certain learners, however, extrinsic rewards in the form of tokens, points, privileges, and removal of unpleasant tasks can help associate learning with pleasant experiences.

## Goals

Adult learners' readiness to learn increases when they need to achieve a particular goal and can immediately apply the new knowledge or skills to real-life situations.

## Experience

Adult learners bring a wealth of experience with them to any learning program. That experience becomes a resource for learning. Whenever possible, instruction should link new material to a learner's existing knowledge to create a powerful and relevant learning experience. Because adults learn best by doing, many training sessions use ***experiential learning*** to help adults learn a skill by doing it in a real or simulated environment. In experiential learning, participants first encounter a problem that figuratively or literally places them in a real-world experience. By responding to the problem, learners discover key learning points. A briefing that follows, elicits, and reinforces those learning points. The initial problem can take many forms, such as a simulation or case study. Experiential learning is popular for teaching skills in which learners must make judgment, for example, in teaching management skills where decision making is integral to the job.

## Culture

How are decision makers and prospective training participants used to doing things? What values, rituals, and shared or different points of view must be reflected and respected in the instructional design? When designing training, the WLP professional needs to account for these cultural differences, which encompass both organizational culture and international culture. For example, if the learning audience consists primarily of machinists, the WLP professional may need to modify a learning design with a heavy emphasis on lecture to include more hands-on, interactive components. Solomon (2004) lists several organizational cultures that can affect training design:

- safety-oriented
- quality-oriented
- ethical
- technology-driven
- innovative
- customer service
- compassionate
- team
- constructive
- passive-defensive
- aggressive-defensive-competitive.

The training designer should also note that organizational cultures can vary from department to department within the same organization. For example, a sales department may be far more competitive and individualistic than a research and development department within the same organization.

International, or otherwise highly diverse, contexts also present a variety of cultural variables that affect training design. Craig (1996) describes the work of Geert Hofstede, who identified a range of cultural variables in international contexts, including power distance. Power distance describes how much emphasis a society places on differences in status and authority in terms of formality of relationships, dependency of learners, strict adherence to guidelines, and conformity. In a high-power distance culture—characterized by highly formal relationships, dependent learners, emphasis on teachers over learners, fixed approach to learning, and conformity to guidelines—the WLP professional may have to adjust the training design to explicitly encourage learner initiative and participation.

# Theories of Learning and Memory

Basically, learning is change and adaptation. Humans have an enormous capacity for learning. This learning capability permits people to change as they receive information from the environment. Learning is an innate capability in all humans that varies by individual. The most adaptable individuals, especially in primitive times, learned more rapidly than others about the opportunities and dangers surrounding them, and they passed this learning ability on to their offspring. Given this definition of learning as change—the ability to adapt to new information—the job of the WLP professional is to help people learn, to help them change.

This section outlines theories of how learners deal with and internalize various stimuli to increase the success of instruction. WLP professionals must understand how humans access, treat, and retrieve what is transmitted to them to increase the probability of successful learning transfer and retention. Some important theories of learning and memory include behaviorism and cognitivism.

## Behaviorism

As noted by Karmlinger and Huberty (1990), behaviorists are concerned with discovering the relationship between stimuli and responses to predict and control behavior. The approach is based on the premise that learning occurs primarily through the reinforcement of desired responses.

The watchword is "reward." Behaviorists are more interested in discovering the external controls that affect internal processes and less concerned with mental processes. The objective is to shape behavior through reinforcement and get the learner to internalize the reinforcement so that new behavior is rewarding in itself.

As Karmlinger and Huberty point out, the first application of behaviorism to instructional design came with the programmed learning movement. B.F. Skinner, an American behaviorist, was chiefly interested in learning processes. He used reinforcement to successfully teach pigeons to bowl. Simply, if a pigeon moved the ball toward the pins, it got a piece of grain; if not, it didn't.

He applied laboratory findings to complex forms of human learning using a technique called programmed learning. In this technique, the information to be learned is broken down into small steps. At each step, a single new term or idea is introduced, and material previously covered is reviewed. Learners respond to each step in a manner appropriate to the instruction, for example by answering a question or filling in a blank. The learner is immediately told whether the answer is right or wrong. As the learner progresses through the programmed materials, his or her behavior is gradually shaped until the learning objective is achieved.

Techniques of behaviorism include prompting, cueing, behavioral modeling, simulations, role play, skill drills, and positive reinforcement.

## Cognitivism

According to Karmlinger and Huberty (1990), the cognitive approach is an academic approach based on the principle that learning occurs primarily through exposure to logically presented information. Cognitive psychologists are interested in the organization of memory and thinking. Cognitivism represents a shift from a focus on behavior to an interest in the organization of memory and thinking. For cognitive scientists, the basic model of the mind is an information-processing system. They do not focus on stimuli and responses but rather on interest in more holistic, internal processes (for example, problem solving, comprehension, and so forth).

Instructional systems design (ISD) has adopted many of the strategies developed by the cognitive science movement. The most important of these strategies is making a distinction between novices and experts, especially when analyzing tasks and designing and evaluating instruction.

Karmlinger and Huberty (1990) point out that cognitivism is the "tell" approach to learning; its predominant learning activity is the lecture. In the 1990s, however, the trend ran to shorter mini-lectures geared to a television culture.

The techniques of cognitivism include diagrams, films, panels, interviews with subject matter experts (SMEs), class presentations, readings, debates, and case studies.

### Advantages of Behaviorism and Cognitivism

Behaviorism

- sets up objectives that are clear and unmistakable
- ensures behavioral practice, not just theory
- works best for helping learners to acquire behavioral skills
- is highly specific
- is observable (learners know when they have succeeded).

Cognitivism

- is faster than other methods
- treats people as adults
- doesn't waste people's time
- builds up a base of information, concepts, and rules
- provides the rationale upon which action is based.

# The Learning Brain Model

There has been a great deal of research done on right- and left-brain behaviors. Most people think with both sides of the brain, but have a strong preference to think with one side or the other. Although the two hemispheres of the brain process information differently, they are complementary rather than competitive. For example, problem-solving taps into both sides. The left side analyzes the problem, whereas the right develops alternative solutions. To make a decision, the left side compares the solutions with the initial problem, whereas the right side evaluates the solutions in terms of the overall situation. Real power comes from combining the two; when the right and left sides of the brain are combined, long-term learning occurs. This model asserts that the different sides of the brain handle different types of input. The specialized functions of the left side of the brain include

- time orientation
- sequential processing of events
- language skills
- logic
- mathematics
- analysis
- awareness of cause and effect.

The specialized functions of the right side of the brain include

- emotion
- intuition
- visual-spatial orientation
- music
- art, imagery, and pattern awareness
- synthesis of information
- simultaneous processing of events
- timelessness
- divergent thinking.

W.E. (Ned) Herrmann (1988), who pioneered the study of the brain in the field of business—specifically, how individuals' thinking preferences, or brain dominance, affect the way they work, learn, and communicate—combined several brain models into a four-quadrant model.

Each quadrant models a different type of information processing. These are the four quadrants:

- **Upper-left cerebral:** These thinkers are logical, analytical, mathematical, technical, and quantitative. They usually think in words and numbers. They learn by acquiring and quantifying facts, using analysis and logic, building cases, and forming theories.

- **Lower-left limbic:** These thinkers are controlled, conservative, organized, administrative, sequential, and procedural. They think in terms of rules and learn by organizing and structuring information, sequencing content, evaluating skills through practice, and implementing course content.

- **Upper-right cerebral:** These thinkers are visual, creative, synthesizing, artistic, conceptual, and holistic. Generally, they are risk takers and entrepreneurs. They usually think in images and learn by taking initiative, exploring possibilities, relying on intuition and self-discovery, constructing concepts, and synthesizing content.

- **Lower-right limbic:** These thinkers are interpersonal, emotional, musical, and spiritual. They think in terms of feelings. They learn by listening and sharing ideas, integrating experiences with self, moving and feeling, getting emotionally involved, and harmonizing with the content. To be effective, learning programs should address the various ways individuals take in and process information.

## Accelerated Learning

The purpose of accelerated learning is to involve both the right and left hemispheres and the cortex and limbic systems of the brain in learning. By involving the different functions, learning is made more natural. Several principles are involved in accelerated learning:

- **Affective state:** The brain chemistry of a positive state of the nervous system differs from that of a fearful and angry state. Stressful environments cause the brain to downshift naturally. Eliminating excess stress, fear of failure, and negativity greatly enhances the learner's receptivity to training.

- **Beliefs toward learning:** Many people believe that learning is difficult—a belief that can be altered. Learning is one of the most joyful and natural aspects of being human. Unfortunately, many people have a diminished view of their intelligence, learning abilities, and performance potential. Many people underachieve not because of a lack of intelligence, but because of an insufficient belief in their ability or power to learn or to accomplish some task. Henry Ford put it succinctly: "Whether you believe you can or you believe you can't, you're right." Techniques exist to help learners govern their beliefs and attitudes.

- **Information networks:** Information is recorded in vast, interconnecting neural networks. Provisions for connecting new material to content learned previously and applying new material back on the job increase the integration and retention of learning. A global context for the learning material makes learning easier.

- ***Nonconscious learning:*** As much as 80 percent of learning may be nonconscious. Accelerated learning techniques work with more of the mind, maximizing people's natural potential for learning.

- ***Learning cycles:*** A learner's attention cycles require restimulation of an optimal learning state through changes of pace. Shorter segments are better processed and retained than longer, continuous learning segments.

- ***Multisensory input:*** Learners have different learning styles. Individuals have many different ways of processing information and experiences through the visual, auditory, and kinesthetic senses. Providing multisensory instruction enhances information processing through greater stimulation and provides reinforcement through other channels.

- ***Learning readiness state:*** A calm, relaxed state—physically and mentally—is the optimum state for peak learning. In a relaxed state, the brain produces steady alpha rhythms, one of four types of brain waves. The types of brain waves correspond to different mental states. Alpha waves characterize a calm but alert state conducive to rapid assimilation of information. In the alpha state, learning happens effortlessly.

Like all other learning, accelerated learning should be applied only in situations in which performers have a documented skill and knowledge gap. Accelerated learning programs only worsen problems that are the result of a lack of proper motivation, tools, or processes.

## Neurolinguistic Programming and Modes of Learning

For years, studies on how people prefer to get new information have been conducted in the field of neurolinguistic programming. Learners distinguish between external experience (information received from the environment through the five senses) and internal experience (what happens inside).

These studies have found that learner preferences fall into three categories, often referred to as the VAK model:

- ***visual:*** intake by seeing

- ***auditory:*** intake by hearing

- ***kinesthetic:*** intake by doing and touching.

People vary in their orientation toward these three categories. Some people intake information primarily through one mode of learning, whereas others use a combination of all three. Intake styles are not the same as intelligence. Whether a person prefers to learn by seeing, hearing, or doing has no bearing on how intelligent he or she is. Intake preferences are simply an individual's preferred method for receiving new information, and those preferences determine how learners assimilate, sort, retain, retrieve, and reproduce new information.

Visual learners, for example, prefer pictures, diagrams, and other visuals. They probably need to see something to know it. They may have an artistic ability and a strong sense of color. They may have difficulty following directions or learning from lectures. They may overreact to noise or misinterpret words.

Auditory learners, however, prefer to get information by listening. They need to hear something to know it. They may have difficulty following written directions or any activity that includes reading.

Finally, kinesthetic learners prefer hands-on learning. They need to do something to know it. They assemble things without reading directions and usually have good spatial perception. They learn best when they are actively involved.

So how do these learning style preferences affect the design of learning? Instructional designers need to strive to create a variety of approaches that use techniques and activities that engage all learning preferences.

## External and Environmental Influences

As a group, adult learners vary greatly in their education, background, experience, intelligence, emotional stability, and motivation for achievement. When preparing for learning, WLP professionals should be aware that many external and environmental factors influence learning. For example, the learning environment may have an effect on facilitating learning. Adults learn well in environments that are more informal than the traditional classroom. For example, a U-shaped seating arrangement and refreshments may create a more relaxed atmosphere. Setting goals and expectations helps to orient learners, stimulate their motivation, and leverage life experiences to make the connection between new knowledge and background information they may have.

Other factors that may influence a participant's ability to learn include

- stress and time pressures
- job status
- learning environment
- peers
- supervisor
- family situation
- company conditions.

## Multiple Intelligences

Whereas intake and learning styles reflect how people prefer to receive information, intelligence reflects how they process information. Howard Gardner, from Harvard University, has been challenging the basic beliefs about intelligence since the early 1980s. Gardner suggests that intelligence is more multifaceted than has been thought and that traditional measures, such as intelligence quotient (IQ) tests, do not accurately measure all its facets. He also says intelligence is not fixed. He defines intelligence as

- a measurable aptitude

- an aptitude that people use to create and solve problems

- an aptitude valued by the culture.

In *Frames of Mind* (1983), Gardner describes his initial list of intelligences. In 1987, he added three additional intelligences to his list and said he expects the list to continue to grow. The intelligences are

- ***interpersonal:*** aptitude for working with others

- ***logical/mathematical:*** aptitude for math, logic, and deduction

- ***spatial/visual:*** aptitude for picturing and seeing

- ***musical:*** aptitude for musical expression

- ***linguistic/verbal:*** aptitude for the written or spoken word

- ***intrapersonal:*** aptitude for working alone

- ***bodily/kinesthetic:*** aptitude for being physical

- ***emotional:*** aptitude for identifying emotion

- ***naturalistic:*** aptitude for being with nature

- ***existential:*** aptitude for understanding one's purpose.

Gardner believes that most people are comfortable in three to four of these intelligences and avoid the others. For example, for learners who are not comfortable working with others, doing group case studies may interfere with their ability to process new material. Video-based instruction is not good for people with lower spatial and visual aptitudes. People with strong bodily and kinesthetic aptitudes need to move around while they are learning. Awareness of different intelligences can enable the designer to create training that will enable more learners to engage with the material and thus successfully learn it.

## ✓ Chapter 1 Knowledge Check

1.  **A WLP professional is tailoring instructional materials to the leadership training needs of her executives. This is an example of**

    __ A.  The application of adult learning theory in designing instruction

    __ B.  Objective-centered instruction

    __ C.  The learning brain model of instruction

    __ D.  How the VAK model can be applied to improving adult learning

2.  **When a WLP professional focuses identifying observable and measurable outcomes for his training on ethics and business conduct, which theory of learning and instruction is being applied?**

    __ A.  Subjective-centered

    __ B.  Objective-centered

    __ C.  Experience-centered

    __ D.  Opportunity-centered

3.  **Which of the following best describes the reasons that Maslow's hierarchy of needs is important in relation to adult learning?**

    __ A.  Adult learners learn differently from children, and five key principles affect how adults learn: self-concept, prior experience, readiness to learn, orientation to learning, and motivation.

    __ B.  To predict and control behavior, stimuli are linked to responses. The approach is based on the premise that learning occurs primarily through reinforcement of desired responses—meaning "rewards."

    __ C.  In this didactic model, someone "telling" the information leads a formal learning session—usually in lecture format.

    __ D.  Five levels of needs indicate that a person can achieve a higher level of need only after lower levels are satisfied, which suggests that people are motivated by different factors—factors that may be unknown or difficult to discern.

4.  **In the field of workplace learning and performance, what is Malcolm Knowles's key contribution to adult learning?**

    __ A.  Andragogy

    __ B.  Pedagogy

    __ C.  The whole brain

    __ D.  Accelerated learning

**5.  Which of the following is *not* an adult learning characteristic based on the andragogy model?**

___ A.  As people mature, they develop a psychological need to be self-directed.

___ B.  As people mature, they accumulate experience and knowledge, which becomes a resource for learning.

___ C.  As people mature, their readiness to learn is directly related to age level and curriculum.

___ D.  As people mature, their motivation to learn becomes increasingly internal.

**6.  Adult development theories are concerned with**

___ A.  How adults change as they age and the effect on learning

___ B.  How adults' motivation becomes more internalized as they age and the effect on learning

___ C.  How adults think with both sides of their brains but have a strong preference for one side or the other

___ D.  How adults have learning preferences that fall into the three categories visual, auditory, and kinesthetic

**7.  A new sales training program focused on improving the motivation of the sales force is most likely to focus on which of the following Bloom categories of learning?**

___ A.  Knowledge

___ B.  Skills

___ C.  Attitude

___ D.  Competencies

**8.  Which of the following guidelines did Carl Rogers describe as a critical element to remember in adult learning situations?**

___ A.  Instructional designers may need to adjust training designs for cultural differences.

___ B.  Adult learners' readiness to learn increases when they need to achieve a particular goal and can immediately apply the new knowledge or skills to real-life situations.

___ C.  Adults bring a wealth of experience with them to any learning.

___ D.  Facilitators establish the initial mood or climate of the class experience and clarify the purpose of the individuals in the class as well as more general purposes of the group.

9. **Which of the following theories of learning focuses on matching individual needs to appropriate instructional experiences and is particularly useful for helping employees adapt to changes in their work lives?**

    \_\_ A.  Subjective-centered

    \_\_ B.  Objective-centered

    \_\_ C.  Experience-centered

    \_\_ D.  Opportunity-centered

10. **Cognitivism is an approach based on the principle that**

    \_\_ A.  Adults learn most effectively when learning is organized by cognitive, psychomotor, and affective outcomes starting from the simplest behavior and ranging to the most complex

    \_\_ B.  Adults are concerned with discovering the relationship between stimuli and responses in order to predict and control behavior

    \_\_ C.  Learning occurs primarily through exposure to logically presented information and is interested in the organization of memory and thinking

    \_\_ D.  Learning needs change as adults mature

11. **Which learning theory seeks to involve the right and left hemispheres of the brain and the cortex and limbic systems in learning—and by involving the different functions makes learning more natural?**

    \_\_ A.  Andragogy

    \_\_ B.  Accelerated learning

    \_\_ C.  Multiple intelligences

    \_\_ D.  The four-quadrant model

12. **According to the VAK model, when designing learning for kinesthetic learners, which of the following should be included based on their preferred mode of learning?**

    \_\_ A.  Visuals such as pictures and diagrams

    \_\_ B.  Lectures

    \_\_ C.  Hands-on activities

    \_\_ D.  Music

**13. Which of the following theories and models is associated with Howard Gardner?**

   __ A.  Multiple intelligences

   __ B.  Hierarchy of needs

   __ C.  Neurolinguistic programming

   __ D.  Accelerated learning

# References

Anderson, L.W., D.R. Krathwohl, and P.W. Airasian, et al. (2000). *Taxonomy for Learning, Teaching, and Assessing, A: A Revision of Bloom's Taxonomy of Educational Objectives*. New York: Longman.

Aslanian, C.B., and H.M. Brickell. (1980). *Americans in Transition: Life Changes as Reasons for Adult Learning*. New York: College Entrance Examination Board.

Biech, E. (2005). *Training for Dummies®*. Hoboken, NJ: Wiley Publishing.

Bridges, W. (1980). *Transitions*. Reading, MA: Addison-Wesley.

Brim, O.G. (1968). "Adult Socialization and Society." In J. Clausen, ed., *Socialization and Society*. Boston: Little, Brown.

Brim, O.G., and C.D. Ryff. (1980). "On the Properties of Life Events." In R. Baltes and O.G. Brim, eds., *Life-Span Development and Behavior*. Volume 3. New York: Academic Press.

Brookfield, S. (1987). *Developing Critical Thinkers*. San Francisco: Jossey-Bass.

Carliner, S. (2002). *Designing E-Learning*. Alexandria, VA: ASTD Press.

——— . (2003). *Training Design Basics*. Alexandria, VA: ASTD Press.

Craig, R.L., ed. (1996). *The ASTD Training and Development Handbook*. 4th edition. New York: McGraw-Hill.

Daloz, L.A. (1986). *Effective Teaching and Mentoring: Realizing the Transformational Power of Adult Learning Experiences*. San Francisco: Jossey-Bass.

Fairbanks, D.M. (1992). "Accelerated Learning." *Infoline* No. 259209.

Gardner, H. (1983). *Frames of Mind: The Theory of Multiple Intelligences*. New York: Basic Books.

Herrmann, W.E. (1988). *The Creative Brain*. Lake Lure, NC: Brain Books.

Hultsch, D.F., and J.K. Plemons. (1979). "Life Events and Life Span Development." In P. Baltes and O.G. Brim, eds., *Life-Span Development and Behavior*. Volume 2. New York: Academic Press.

Jacobsen, S. (1994). "Neurolinguistic Programming." *Infoline* No. 259404. (Out of print.)

Jarvis, P. (1987). *Adult Learning in the Social Context*. London: Croom Helm.

Jorz, J., and L. Oliver. (1985). "How to Create a Good Learning Environment." *Infoline* No. 258506.

Karmlinger, T., and T. Huberty. (December 1990). "Behaviorism Versus Humanism." *Training & Development Journal*, pp. 41–45.

Knowles, M. (1984). *The Adult Learner: A Neglected Species.* 3rd edition. Houston, TX: Gulf Publishing.

Knowles, M., E.S. Holton III, and R.A. Swanson. (2005). *The Adult Learner.* 6th edition. Burlington, MA: Elsevier.

Maresh, N. (2000). "Breathing Life Into Adult Learning." In G. Piskurich, P. Beckschi, and B. Hall, eds., *The ASTD Handbook of Training Design and Delivery.* New York: McGraw-Hill.

Maslow, A. (1954). *Motivation and Personality.* New York: Harper.

McArdle, G.E. (1999). *Training Design and Delivery.* Alexandria, VA: ASTD Press.

Merriam, S.B. (1984). *Adult Development: Implications for Adult Education.* Columbus, OH: ERIC Clearinghouse on Adult, Career, and Vocational Education.

Merriam, S.B., and R.S. Caffarella. (1991). *Learning in Adulthood.* San Francisco: Jossey-Bass.

Neugarten, B. (1976). "Adaptation and the Life Cycle." *Counseling Psychologist,* 6, pp. 16-20.

———. (1979). "Time, Age, and the Life Cycle." *American Journal of Psychiatry,* pp. 136, 887-893.

Neugarten, B., and N. Datan. (1973). "Sociological Perspectives on the Life Cycle." In P. Baltes and K.W. Schaie, eds., *Life-Span Development Psychology: Personality and Socialization.* New York: Academic Press.

Piskurich, G. (2003). *Trainer Basics.* Alexandria, VA: ASTD Press.

Reynolds, A. (1993). *The Trainer's Dictionary: HRD Terms, Acronyms, Initials, and Abbreviations.* Amherst, MA: HRD Press.

Rhinesmith, S.H. (1996). "Training for Global Operations." In R.L. Craig, ed. *The ASTD Training and Development Handbook.* 4th edition. New York: McGraw-Hill.

Russell, S. (1998). "Training and Learning Styles." *Infoline* No. 258804.

Russo, C.S., ed. (2003). "Basic Training for Trainers." *Infoline* No. 258808.

Russo, C., and J. Mitchell, eds. (2005). "The *Infoline* Dictionary of Basic Trainer Terms." *Infoline* No. 250513.

Sanders, E.S., and S. Thiagarajan. (2001). *Performance Intervention Maps.* Alexandria, VA: ASTD Press.

Sharpe, C. ed. (1997). "Course Design and Development." *Infoline* No. 258905.

———. (1997). "How to Motivate Employees." *Infoline* No. 259108. (out of print)

Solomon, C. (2004). "Culture Audits: Supporting Organizational Success." *Infoline* No. 250412.

Stolovitch, H.D., and E.J. Keeps. (2002). *Telling Ain't Training*. Alexandria, VA: ASTD Press.

Whitbourne, S., and C. Weinstock. (1979). *Adult Development*. New York: Holt, Rinehart & Winston.

# 2
# Instructional Design Theory and Process

From the perspective of an instructional designer, any undertaking that includes a learner and the subject matter necessary to learn requires an instructional system. Instructional designers need inputs like subject matter and resources, an Instructional Systems Design (ISD) process, and outputs like curriculum and materials to build a training course. This combination of elements is called an *instructional system*. Anything from a lecture to web-based training starts with the same fundamentals.

Instructional designers use many theories and models to design instruction. One of the most fundamental models is the ADDIE (analysis, design, development, implementation, and evaluation) model, or some variation of it, which provides designers with the necessary structure for designing any curriculum, regardless of the instructional methods employed. The relevant theme in all that is available is that learning and performance professionals use a systematic process that includes analysis, design, development, implementation, and evaluation.

Upon this foundation, instructional designers then design and develop courses—a task that includes developing objectives and creating evaluation tasks.

## Learning Objectives:

- ☑ Describe the ADDIE model for designing instruction.

- ☑ List Gagne's nine instructional events.

- ☑ Define the key differences among the Dick and Carey, Seels and Glasgow, and Smith and Ragan approaches to ISD.

- ☑ Define accelerated learning.

- ☑ Describe how courses are designed.

- ☑ Discuss Mager's influence on the WLP profession.

- ☑ Discuss the theories of rapid instructional design and learner-centered instruction.

- ☑ Detail how Bloom's taxonomy aids WLP professionals in identifying the skills, knowledge, and attitudes to be learned during the instructional design process.

- ☑ Describe two types of objectives and the components of writing learning objectives in the A-B-C-D format.

# Principles Guiding Training Design

Although WLP professionals have a wide variety of learning solutions to choose from, one of the first steps in the instructional design process includes conducting a needs analysis to ensure that the what is needed can in fact be remedied with training.

When new course designers and developers first start a project, many immediately rush to work on slides, quizzes, student workbooks, and similar material. After all, sponsors often provide course designers and developers with the particulars: the audience, the material that the course needs to cover, and the completion date for the project.

Although sponsors provide this information about projects, it might not be complete enough for instructional design purposes. It might be correct. However, it might reflect an incomplete understanding of the learners or the content.

When starting a learning project, the instructional designer's first task is to verify the information he or she has received and fill in any missing pieces through analysis. To get started, instructional designers need to understand and know the

- sponsor's request
- business need underlying the project
- desired performance
- tasks involved in performance
- learners and the influences on them
- constraints on the project.

In addition, the designer needs to be aware of some fundamental principles that underpin the design and development of learning.

## Produce Measurable Improvements in Human Behavior

If the purpose of training is to help make workers measurably more effective in their work, then practitioners must specifically identify the behaviors that should improve and how to measure those behaviors before work begins on the training program. After workers complete the training program, learning professionals should follow the performance of learners on the job and measure changes in on-the-job behavior.

Furthermore, improvements in behavior must offer tangible benefits to the organization sponsoring the training. Ideally, these tangible benefits are financial. For example, if workers produce more widgets per hour, organizations have more widgets to sell. Or, if learners reduce the number of errors in their work, organizations reduce the cost of re-work. But sometimes, benefits are intangible, such as more empathetic customer service. Such changes often lead to financial rewards, too. For example, better customer service can result in improved retention of customers.

# Performance Improvements: Ensure That Training Is Appropriate Solution

Taking a training class alone does not always result in measurable changes in workplace behavior. This happens because training addresses only one of the six drivers of performance: skills and knowledge. In some instances, workers *do* have the skills and knowledge to handle a task but still do not perform the task effectively. In such situations, another factor affects performance. That factor might be one of the following:

- *A lack of motivation:* Even if workers have the skills, knowledge, and resources to do their jobs, a lack of motivation can negatively affect performance. Consider an example of consultants who do not generate new sales leads while they are working in the field. If skills and knowledge are the source of the problem, they may not generate leads because they lack sales training. However, if workers are compensated for the number of productive hours in the field and receive no compensation for generating new leads, they will not be motivated to generate new sales. Solving this problem requires changes in reward and compensation systems rather than training.

- *A lack of tools or resources needed to perform the task:* Suppose workers receive training on new word processing software, but the software has not yet been installed on their computers. The workers cannot perform the skills learned in the training course because they do not have the software resources on which to practice the skills.

- *An inadequate or nonexistent structure or process:* In the case of the rude customer service representatives, the problem could be strict time limits on calls. When customer service representatives exceed that time limit, they are reprimanded. As a result, representatives abruptly end calls with customers to avoid being reprimanded by their supervisors. Solving this problem would require removing the limit on the length of calls.

- *A lack of information:* Lack of information can also create performance gaps. Consider the example of a person whose reports are consistently late. Sending that person to a writing class will not solve the problem if the reason that he always delivers them late is that he lacks access to the information he needs to write the reports.

- *A lack of health:* Consider an employee on a production line who has been making an increasing number of errors. Sending this person to training will not solve the problem because he or she already has the skills to carry out the tasks. However, recent layoffs may have caused an increase in the number of hours that he or she is required to work, resulting in increased stress and perhaps reduced sleep, which may be the cause of the increase in errors.

Because some solutions for improving performance do not require training courses, they are sometimes called **interventions** by performance specialists. Using this term often helps WLP professionals keep an open mind about the approach they take. If the performance problem results from a lack of skills and knowledge, a training course may be the appropriate solution. If the poor performance is due to a lack of motivation, information, or resources, inadequate or faulty processes and systems, or a health issue, the solution is then found through different answers.

# Theories and Models for Designing Instruction

ISD is a systems approach to creating instruction. It may also be called instructional development (ID), curriculum development (CD), instructional systems for training (IST), or a variety of other terms. The differences among the many systems are usually modest in scope and tend to be linked to terminology and procedural issues.

ISD is based on the idea that training is most effective when it provides learners with a clear statement of what they must be able to do as a result of training and how their performance will be evaluated. The program is then designed to teach the skills through hands-on practice or performance-based instruction.

The advantages of using an instructional system are numerous, the most important being the ability to design projects quickly and efficiently. Nothing is left to chance or ignored when a designer stays within the framework of the ADDIE or other ISD models. One possible disadvantage is the necessity of a designer to be familiar with the ISD process. ISD works so well because it produces observable, measurable, and replicable elements. These elements include analytical methods, objectives, evaluation schemes, design plans, and other components.

Although ISD is a system, it is not so rigid that it lacks flexibility. In fact, the more instructional designers work with ISD, the more they realize that the system allows many opportunities to be creative.

## The ADDIE Model

Several ISD models are named after individuals and institutions; however, the ADDIE model is based on and named after five elements of ISD: analysis, design, development, implementation, and evaluation. Most instructional designers use the ADDIE model or some variation of it as the basis for their work. The model is illustrated in Figure 2-1.

In the ADDIE model, analysis is the *input* for the system; design, development, and evaluation are the *process*; and implementation is the *output*. These elements overlap somewhat, depending on the project. More on each component of ADDIE follows.

### Analysis

The terms *analysis* and *assessment* are often used interchangeably by learning and performance professionals. With regard to ISD, analysis is the process of gathering data to identify specific needs—the who, what, where, when, and why of the design process. Just as A is the first letter in the English alphabet, analysis should be the first item addressed in instructional design. Analysis is done for one reason—to find out what learners need to know to be successful.

## Figure 2-1. The ADDIE Instructional Design Model

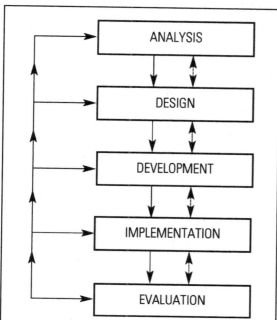

Analysis is the data-gathering phase of instructional design. In this phase, instructional designers assemble information about the project before they consider anything else. Decisions about every aspect of the project must eventually be made. The information that instructional designers gather will be put to use throughout the system, which means that they must have every scrap of data they can get to ensure the design will be successful.

Instructional designers carry out analysis to determine the training needs of an organization, a department, or an individual. The first step for the designer is to think about the people he or she is trying to serve with the training. Is it the entire organization, a department, or an individual? In this phase, designers must identify

- whether a problem exists that training can appropriately address
- the goals and objectives the training should have
- the resources that are available for the project
- the audience that requires the training and its needs (population profiles)
- all additional data needed to successfully complete the project.

The first question to ask in analysis is critical to the success of any training endeavor: "Can the problem be reasonably remedied by training?" Many a novice designer has turned enthusiasm into disaster by assuming that a problem was training related and later discovering that no appreciable change took place in the target population because the cure was not training but some other solution. Although this approach may seem obvious, asking this question should always be the first step in the process.

These are other first-step analysis issues to consider:

- *A target population profile:* Such a profile includes every variable that might affect outcomes, including education levels, cultural influences, language skills, learning styles, levels of participant motivation, organizational politics, and relevant past experience with the subject matter.

- **Types of training:** Preliminary categorization of the types of training helps to narrow the range of options available for instructional design. This should not be confused with training platforms (see next entry). Types of training include skills enhancement, technical, marketing, managerial, cross-cultural, sensitivity, organizational change, literacy, and traditional academic.

- **Training platforms:** Training platforms are the delivery systems for training. Examples include classroom training, on-the-job training, multimedia approaches, computer-based training, distance learning, teleconferencing, and seminars.

- **Resources:** The resources available for the project might include access to SMEs; sources of print materials, including manuals, books, videos, and other reference materials; funds procurable for the project; existing courseware and materials; facilitators on hand for implementation; and support equipment, such as overhead projectors and video playback equipment.

- **Constraints:** These are issues that might cause problems, including unreasonable deadlines; limited access to training facilities; platform-related deficiencies, including broken or aging equipment; and anything else that can influence a project's success or failure.

A number of methods are used during the analysis phase to gather and review data, including surveys, focus groups, materials review, SME panels, and existing programs review. Data-collection techniques are discussed in greater detail in Chapter 7, "Assessment Methods and Formats," and Chapter 11, "Research Methods."

## Design

Design is the blueprinting stage of instructional systems during which instructional designers create the blueprint with all the specifications necessary to complete the project. In this phase, the designer provides the basic foundation and structure for the training project. The foundation consists of goals, objectives, and evaluation tasks that must be developed and their sequence. The structure is based on the many decisions that must be made regarding training platforms and other implementation questions. A key output of this phase includes the design plan.

In this phase, the designer will

- prepare instructional objectives
- develop instructional evaluation techniques and tasks
- develop a program evaluation plan
- develop the sequence and structure of the course
- prepare logic and objective maps
- determine and prepare draft copies of the necessary materials.

A key output of this phase includes the design plan, in which the designer should include a working map for the project. This plan serves as the blueprint for developing the training and also lists all of the objectives written for the training program, along with a list of additional items needed. Some examples of the additional items needed include printed materials; scripts and storyboards for computer-based projects; evaluation materials including tests, quizzes, and other formal evaluations; lesson plans; staff assignments and responsibilities; and a project management plan that includes milestones and deadlines.

---

## What Comes First: Budget or Design?

In an ideal world, budget allocation for a course follows the design phase. After this, each course would then receive funds according to anticipated costs and benefits.

Realistically, an organization's budget cycle and funding practices often dictate a course's budget, limiting design and development decisions. Gradually, organizational decision makers are becoming more aware of the value and utility of basing a course's budget on its design, rather than the reverse. However, there is still little logic to the funding of many courses.

Training professionals need to know about organizational budget cycles and funding practices. Besides making formal inquiries, a WLP professional who consults the organizational grapevine may discover what kinds of funding appeals—formal or informal, mostly prose or mostly statistics, early or late in the budget cycle—have been the most successful in the past.

---

### Development

Materials production and pilot testing are the hallmarks of development. At this stage, most nondesigners begin to see progress. Everything from lecture notes to virtual reality moves from design to deliverable. A key step before instructional designers move from development to implementation is pilot testing to ensure that deliverables do not have to be redeveloped. Because of the time and expense involved, no one wants to reprint materials or recode a technology-based project after a project goes into implementation. The pilot testing process allows organizations to implement any necessary changes before the expenses associated with full-scale materials development are realized. The time and effort expended in pilot testing is well worth the effort, if for this reason alone. Pilot testing also helps designers feel confident that what they have designed works.

In the development phase, the tangible and most easily recognized components of training begin to take shape. The project moves from blueprint to construction using the design plan as a guide. These are some of the major development phase elements:

- All participant and instructor materials are prepared in draft form and reviewed by SMEs and designers for accuracy.

- Nonprint media, such as audio, video, and computer-based programs, are prepared and reviewed.

- Programs are pilot tested; changes are incorporated into the final program, and materials are modified as necessary.

- Programs are packaged and distributed in preparation for implementation.

## Implementation

At implementation, the design plan meets the learner and the content is delivered. The level 1 (reaction) evaluation process that most designers and learners are familiar with takes place at this stage. Evaluation is used to gauge the degree to which learners meet objectives and facilitators or technologies to deliver the project.

In most implementations, learning and performance professionals can expect the following:

- assessment of learners' ability to meet program objectives

- evaluation of program design by facilitators

- review of the materials prepared for the program

- review of implementation-specific elements, such as class size, format, and so on

- modification of design and materials as suggested by evaluation.

## Evaluation

Designers should keep in mind that although the evaluation element of the ADDIE model appears to be the last function, in reality, evaluation takes place at every point throughout the ISD process.

The activities associated with this phase include

- confirming that all subject matter is correct and reviewed by SMEs

- consulting with stakeholders to ensure adherence to established project goals

- adhering to the design plan and procuring sign-off on all critical design elements

- reviewing and acting on all evaluation from participants, facilitators, and other project end users

- ensuring quality control of the process by constant and thorough evaluation of all remaining project elements.

## Gagne's Nine Events of Instruction

Another model with implications for training design is Gagne's nine events of instruction (Gagne, Briggs, and Wager 1988), which relate to the way that instructional designers develop lesson plans. A lesson plan is a sequential set of events that leads to a desired goal. The single most important reason for lesson plans is that training often requires implementation of the same course numerous times. Performing each implementation of the course the same way is essential to ensure conformance to content and quality standards.

Over the years, numerous designs for lesson plans have evolved. Although some designers may claim that certain plans have their roots planted firmly in a theoretical base, most lesson plans are the product of honest efforts to find a way to offer facilitators some assistance in implementing a course.

One significant aspect of learning theory that Gagne, Briggs, and Wager (1988) describe is the formalization of approaches in designing training. The theory supports the notion of an ideal teaching sequence that enables learners to retain the concepts, skills, and procedures taught to them because they are presented in a way that enhances and supports how the mind works.

For years, researchers have been studying how the brain works, especially how it retains information. For instructional designers, "how" is an important question. The essence of a designer's role is making sure that learners leave with demonstrated mastery of objectives. The nine events of instruction join theory and practice in a way that can be used in most design situations.

Gagne built the nine events of instruction based on the work of other theorists who studied the way humans process information and move it from sensing to processing to storing it in short- or long-term memory. The nine steps in this process and each so-called event have an instructional design component that is critical in lesson plan design. The nine events have application in lesson plans beyond delivery modalities. All training must be based on the way the learner processes information, or it just will not work.

These are the nine events of instruction:

1. ***Gain the learner's attention.*** In the beginning of a course, helping a learner focus on the course is critical. Gaining attention may mean setting the tone for the course, however, it also sometimes means turning off outside interference rumbling through a learner's mind. In all cases, the attention-gathering process needs to relate to the topic. Some examples include playing videotapes or audiotapes of one minute or less on the topic or demonstrating a task that participants will learn in the course.

2. ***Share the session objectives.*** Presenting the objectives is a crucial factor in setting the framework for meeting the course objectives. Objectives set the destination so that learners will have a map that shows them where they are going.

3. ***Ask the learners to recall prior learning.*** To create the context for the objectives, facilitators must prime the learners for the new material. In some cases, the recall session may end up being technical to ensure that the participants are ready to move on to the new material. Other times, it may be no more than a simple question or discussion that builds the foundation for the information that follows.

4. ***Deliver content.*** How content is presented has more effect on learners than any other facet of the design. Implementation is about presenting new material in a way that ensures that learners meet objectives. Designers can be creative as long as they balance their creativity with what their analysis has told them about the learners.

5. ***Use methods to enhance understanding (for example, case studies or graphs).*** Instructional designers like to use interactivity when building a course to allow and encourage participation by learners. To be effective, interactivity should not take the form of a question tossed out into a room and batted around until something emerges. Designers need to shape and build momentum to keep the learners engaged. Providing learning guidance is the point at which designers can give the facilitator and learner an opportunity to begin practicing skills or discussing concepts that are critical to meeting lesson objectives.

6. ***Provide an opportunity to practice.*** Enhancing individual performance by allowing learners to practice in a safe environment is the main benefit of eliciting performance. At some point in the lesson or course, learners should be able to test their understanding of the new material. Learners must have an opportunity to both offer and receive information because, until now, learners have been largely on their own, receiving feedback from other learners and the facilitator. Generally, this portion of the training is built around small group activities. By working in pairs or small groups, learners may ask questions that they might not otherwise ask the facilitator.

7. ***Provide feedback.*** Learners have a difficult time making progress if they do not receive any information about how they are doing. Designers must ensure that each learner gets enough feedback about his or her progress to allow correction of any uncertainty or error. Designers have many ways to build this feedback into the course, and each course's specific objective domains, time limitations, difficulty of content, learner variables, and possibly other factors influence the designer's approach. One of the true tests of a good designer is how he or she determines the best feedback scheme for the project.

8. ***Assess performance.*** No learner should leave a training course without undergoing some form of evaluation to assess performance. This does not always mean a test or another formal evaluation; it is usually just a check-off list that ensures that the learner has met the objectives. However, every objective has to be evaluated, or it is not worth having as an objective. Objectives have to match evaluation tasks; it is difficult to match the two if one is missing. Designers must find other ways of providing this feedback if they do not plan to offer an exam. For example, for a training program for sales staff, a designer might have a learner simulate closing a sale with a client.

9. ***Provide job aids or references to ensure transfer to the job (retention and implementation).*** At the close of a learning, instructional designers need

to provide a review for the learners. Learners need to appreciate the progress they have made and realize that they have met the objectives presented to them at the beginning of the course.

Sometimes designers choose to eliminate one or more of these events due to time or other constraints. When designing computer-based or multimedia learning solutions, designing the necessary feedback and interaction steps can be difficult. Designers may then decide that they can reduce the nine events to seven or fewer. Usually, guided learning, performance assessment, and feedback suffer the most. At a minimum, designers should use the nine events as a framework for any type of delivery system to ensure that they are at least considering the ramifications of all these elements in their design.

## Rapid Instructional Design

As described by Thiagarajan (2000), rapid instructional design (RID) is a collection of strategies for quickly producing instructional packages that enable a specific group of learners to achieve a set of specific learning objectives. RID involves alternatives, enhancements, and modifications to the ADDIE model.

In recent years, several practitioners have suggested that the traditional ISD model needs to be upgraded to keep pace with changing demands and resources. The traditional ISD model is an effective approach, but it is only one approach. RID is an eclectic approach that provides a flexible choice of techniques based on the nature of the instructional objective, characteristics of the learners, and context of training.

The selection of appropriate instructional development techniques depends on two types of trade-offs. The first is between the ***design*** and ***delivery*** of instruction. Design involves all the activities undertaken before learners interact with the instructional package in learning; delivery is what happens subsequently. An important principle in RID is that the designer must be able to trade off the resources allocated to these two phases.

For example, if the instructional designer has a high resource level for delivery (SMEs serving as instructors, ample time for instruction, small groups of learners, and alternative instructional materials), he or she can skimp on the design.

By contrast, if the designer has extremely limited resources for the delivery of instruction (nonspecialist instructors, a tight learning schedule, and large groups of learners), he or she needs to allocate extra time and other resources to the design process.

Depending on the context, the designer can and should select the optimum allocation of resources between design and delivery. RID is not a replacement for the traditional ISD model. In certain conditions, application of the ISD model is likely to result in more effective instruction without requiring additional time. RID provides an alternative for when designers are working with tight deadlines, limited budgets, and constantly shifting content.

## Figure 2-2. The Dick and Carey Model

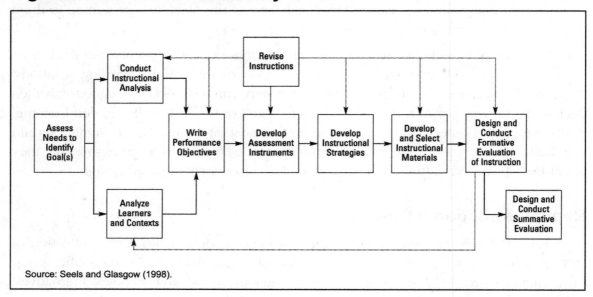

Source: Seels and Glasgow (1998).

## Dick and Carey Systems Approach to Instructional Design

According to Seels and Glasgow (1998), the Dick and Carey (1996) ISD model was presented in a text for instructional designers, which is used extensively in colleges to train instructional designers. Dick and Carey expanded the task analysis step to encompass instructional analysis. In the newest edition (Dick, Carey, and Carey 2004), they added the step of analyzing learners and contexts. The model, illustrated in Figure 2-2, describes the instructional development process from assessing needs to identifying goals through writing objectives to developing materials and evaluating instruction. In particular, they focus on selecting appropriate content for each learning module and organizing the content effectively.

## Seels and Glasgow ISD Model II

The ISD process presented in Barbara Seels and Rita Glasgow's (1998) model, illustrated in Figure 2-3, is based on the assumption that design occurs within the context of project management. Design team members formulate and revise a project management plan as necessary. This plan establishes roles, tasks, timelines, budgets, checkpoints, and supervisory procedures. Team members undertake the steps within the parameters of a project management plan divided into three phases:

1. Needs-analysis management

2. Instructional design management

3. Implementation and evaluation management

## Figure 2-3. The Seels and Glasgow ISD Model II

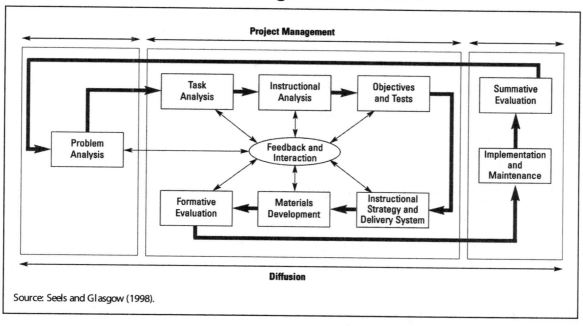

Source: Seels and Glasgow (1998).

Diffusing, or promoting the adoption and maintenance of the project, is an ongoing process. Members of the design team may change depending on the phase in process.

## Smith and Ragan Systematic Instructional Design Model

As noted by Seels and Glasgow (1998), according to the Smith and Ragan ISD model (2004), the designer goes through a three-stage process: analysis, strategy development, and evaluation. (See Figure 2-4.) Smith and Ragan believe these three stages are common to most instructional design models. They qualify their model by cautioning that although designers usually follow the stages in the order listed, circumstances can cause the designer to modify the sequence or to do steps concurrently. Their model differs in that test items are written within the analysis stage right after tasks are analyzed. They also stress the iterative nature of design, which results in constant revision.

## Accelerated Learning

Michael Treacy and Fred Wiersema (1995) noted in their book *The Discipline of Market Leaders* that, because of the constantly changing world of new technology and business, business people have a hard time keeping up. To keep up with rapid changes and the persistent lack of time, instructional designers need to change their strategy. Instead of trying to enable learners to learn harder, they need to learn better.

Accelerated learning helps people build a structure that focuses on the concept of personal mastery described by Peter Senge (1990) in *The Fifth Discipline*. Increased learning capacity lowers stress, reduces conflicts, and builds self-esteem. In contrast, ineffective learning increases stress, triggers blame, and challenges feelings of self-worth.

Accelerated learning stresses that the learning environment—everything from room arrangements to the trainer's attitude—must

- be positive and accepting
- provide a comfortable and colorful setting
- exalt rather than trivialize the learners
- help eliminate or reduce learning barriers
- be supportive of both learners and trainers
- provide a multidimensional approach
- accommodate different learning styles
- make learning fun
- provide for group-based learning
- present material visually as well as verbally.

## Basics of Course Design

Once an instructional designer has identified that a performance gap is due to a lack of skills or knowledge, some type of training is appropriate. One solution might be to create a course. So what do course design and development really mean? Webster says it as well as anyone else:

- ***Design*** is a preliminary sketch or outline showing the main features of something to be executed.

- ***Development*** is the act, process, or result of setting forth and making clear by degrees or in detail.

Course design and development are phases of ISD. In the course design phase, a course designer or design team plans the course, whereas in the development phase, a developer develops the actual training materials for the course. In both phases, the WLP professional makes increasingly precise decisions about what to include in a course and how to convey the content to learners. Several factors guide these decisions:

- ***The audience and what participants need to know:*** The analysis phase determines the KSAs to be learned for satisfactory job or task performance. The KSAs to be learned are written in the form of objectives.

- ***Instructional objectives and focus on learning transfer:*** By focusing on transferring participants' learning to job performance, the training must ultimately lead to better job performance. Otherwise, no matter how entertaining or enlightening it is, the training will fail.

- ***Instructional strategies and effect on the organization:*** The design and development phases spell out the course's expected benefits and costs to the organization. A careful planner keeps costs proportionate to benefits. Course

## Figure 2-4. Smith and Ragan Systematic Instructional Design Model

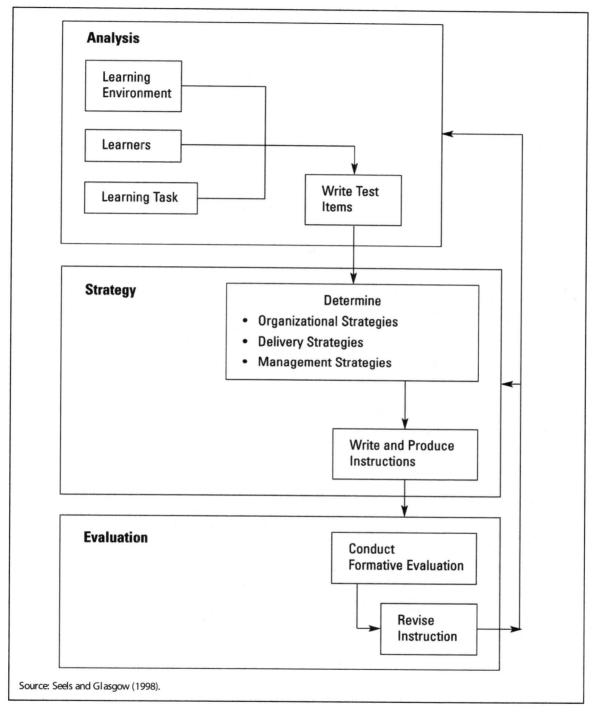

Source: Seels and Glasgow (1998).

design begins with broad planning, moves toward midlevel planning for units or modules (also called the ***mesolevel***), and ends with detailed lesson or learning plans at the micro level. For example, in the design phase, an instructional designer may decide that a film offers the best overview for a course, whereas in the development phase, he or she selects or creates a particular film.

- ***Evaluation:*** For every objective the designer should develop a corresponding evaluation task. Whether the evaluation tasks are formal (for example, taking a test or quiz) or informal (for example, describing a concept), these evaluation components must be determined during the design phase to gauge training effectiveness and performance improvement.

Next, a lesson or plan specifies

- how information will be introduced

- what activity monitors participants' learning

- how information or tasks in one section link with the next training or learning activity.

Throughout design and development, a course designer must constantly assess the value of learning activities and the means for carrying them out by keeping in mind these factors:

- Does the activity enhance participants' motivation to learn?

- How does this activity lead to the desired learning?

- What kind(s) of feedback will evaluate and validate participants' progress in meeting learning objectives?

- Do the activities promote learning retention and transfer of learning to the job?

## Design and Development Teams

Sometimes a solo trainer is responsible for course design and development. Even so, the trainer must consult with other people and with information resources, such as training services or materials directories. Involving training specialists in course design and development is also desirable. So where budgets and time permit, design and development are usually carried out by a team headed by someone from the training department—a course designer.

Teams should consist of people who are knowledgeable or competent in one or more of these areas:

- organizational culture and resources

- adult learning styles

- instructional technology

- matching strategies with course content

- job and occupational analysis
- skills needed for the job
- testing and evaluation.

A course designer often calls on consultants to work on specialized aspects of course design and development. The director may also consult informally with training media and materials suppliers during design and development, but the suppliers are not part of the design and development team—unless a course's primary goal is to acquaint learners with the use of a supplier's product or service. In that case, a supplier representative will likely be on the team.

## Front-End Analysis

Training design should begin only after a fundamental front-end analysis yields a "go" (as opposed to a "no-go") signal. Joe Harless, author of Analyzing Human Performance: Tools for Achieving Business Result (Sharpe 1997), points out that when a performance problem is perceived—by trainers, managers, supervisors, or employees—training may be the solution, only part of the solution, or unrelated to the solution.

Because of this, several questions arise:

- What indicators or symptoms suggest that change is needed?
- What is the root of the problem?
- What role, if any, can training play in remedying the problem?
- What is the monetary value of solving the problem?
- Would an improvement—but less-than-complete remedy—be acceptable?

If training is needed, the analysis phase of ISD continues, and the instructional designer(s) might start sketching out a design while taking into consideration the following resources and constraints: time, money, culture, training population characteristics, availability, and location. Detailed information about how to conduct a needs assessment is provided in Chapter 7, "Assessment Methods and Formats."

## Classes of Objectives

In the front-end or needs analysis, instructional designers gather information about the sponsor's business needs, the desired performance, the tasks learners must master, who the learners are, and the constraints on the project. However, they are not yet ready to begin designing the program. Although the designer has identified the needs and determined what the training program should accomplish, he or she needs to formally state the goals for it. By establishing these goals, both the designer and the sponsor have a common agreement about the purpose of the program.

The single most important skill a designer can learn is how to write objectives. Whether known as **behavioral** or **performance objectives**, or **expected outcomes**, objectives are the keystone of instructional design. An objective must be stated clearly and describe what the learner must be able to do at the end of the specified unit, lesson, course, or program and the conditions under which the learner must do it.

Goals and learning objectives are not the same things. Goals are general statements of desired outcomes, whereas objectives are detailed statements about the outcomes of the learning. For example, a goal might be to improve communications within an organization, which may tie in with an overall business objective. The learning objective for that goal might be

*Given several role-play situations and class discussions, the Better Communications participant should be able to develop at least three specific ways to improve interoffice communications.*

Learning objectives state the content that the proposed training program must cover and the extent to which learners must master the material. Two categories of information gathered in the needs assessment help determine the content that should be covered in the training program. The first of these categories is the desired performance. The second category is the specific tasks learners must master to achieve the desired performance.

The use of learning objectives in curriculum design is identical to the use of a roadmap to show the intended destination and the best way to get there. Objectives are the designation points in curriculum design—without them, learners and designers have no reference point for any single destination.

Training professionals classify learning objectives in many ways, including ***behavioral***, ***performance***, and ***criteria-referenced***, as well as ***terminal*** and ***enabling objectives***. These categories are not necessarily mutually exclusive.

## Mager's Behavioral Learning Objectives

Robert Mager, known for his key contributions to instructional design and his 1962 book, *Preparing Objectives for Programmed Instruction*, influenced school systems for decades and continues to shape corporate training programs today. Mager argued for the use of specific, measurable objectives that both guide designers during courseware development and aid participants in the learning process. These instructional objectives, also known as ***behavioral or performance objectives,*** relate directly to Gagne's second event of instruction, which is to inform learners of objectives.

Behavioral, or performance, objectives are also synonymous with ***criteria-referenced objectives,*** which include provisions for measuring the ability of the learner to meet specific criteria upon completion of learning. According to Mager's work, a learning objective should contain a condition statement, a performance statement, and a criterion statement.

In the design of instructional materials, the instructional designer first analyzes training needs and determines the learning goals of the program. Mager's central concept is that a learning goal should be broken into a subset of smaller tasks or learning objectives. By his definition, a behavioral objective should have three components:

- **Behavior:** The behavior should be specific and observable.
- **Condition:** The conditions under which the behavior is to be completed should be stated and should include the tools or assistance to be provided.
- **Standard:** The desirable level of performance should be stated, including an acceptable range of allowable answers.

## Terminal and Enabling Objectives

Throughout the sequence of instruction, learners work to meet objectives—and to show through various evaluation tasks that they have met the objectives. Another classification of objectives includes course, enabling, and terminal (or performance) objectives. Course objectives state the general purpose(s) or benefit(s) of a course.

As designers distinguish a hierarchy of learning needs in the needs analysis, they also distinguish a hierarchy of objectives when writing them (see Figure 2-5). At the top of the hierarchy are the most important objectives that learners must master. These are often referred to as *main* or *terminal objectives* because these are the ones that learners must master by the time they complete the course. A course typically covers between five and nine terminal objectives.

## Figure 2-5. Example of a Hierarchy of Objectives

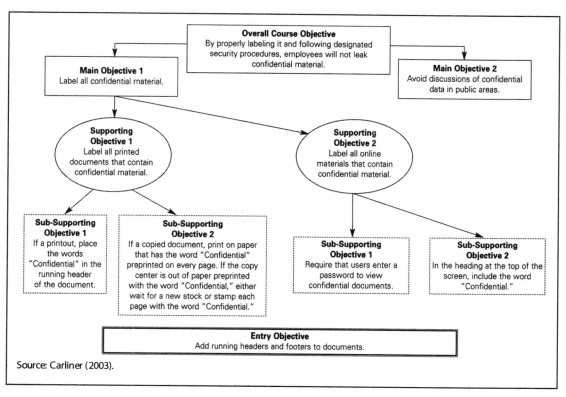

Source: Carliner (2003).

To master one main objective, learners must often master several subordinate ones, called **supporting** or **enabling objectives** because they enable a learner to master the terminal objectives.

Terminal objectives are the final behavioral outcomes of a specific instructional event. The designer must state an objective clearly and describe the intended exit competencies for the specified unit, lesson, course, or program for which it was written. For example, if writing a terminal objective for a unit of instruction in the subject area of learning the Internet, it might look like this:

*Given a computer system, modem, and software, the Internet 101 student should be able to access the Internet and check for any email messages waiting on the system at least five times without error.*

Enabling objectives support the terminal objectives by breaking them down into more manageable chunks. Enabling objectives are the building blocks that provide additional concepts or skills needed to meet the terminal objective. One enabling objective might be

*Given prompts for account name and password, the Internet 101 learner should be able to correctly enter this information without error in five successive attempts.*

## Bloom's Taxonomy and Its Effect on Learning Objectives

As noted by Biech (2005), in the early 1960s, Benjamin Bloom and a university committee identified three learning domains: cognitive, psychomotor, and affective. These domains relate to the terminology that training professionals typically use—knowledge (cognitive), skills (psychomotor), and attitude (affective)—to describe three categories of learning. These are the ultimate goals of the learning process—what the learner acquires as the result of learning.

Bloom's group further expanded on the domains. They created a hierarchical ordering of the cognitive and affective learning outcomes. Their work subdivided each domain, starting from the simplest behavior to the most complex: knowledge, comprehension, application, analysis, synthesis, and evaluation. Each level builds on the earlier one. For example, knowledge must occur prior to comprehension, comprehension must occur prior to application, and so forth. Each level of learning identified the desired specific, observable, and measurable result.

This work is known as Bloom's taxonomy. The divisions are not absolutes, and other systems and hierarchies have been developed since then. Bloom's taxonomy, however, is easily understood and may be the most widely applied. Table 2-1 provides an overview.

Although the committee actually identified three domains of learning, they applied the six levels only to the cognitive and affective learning domains. They did not elaborate on psychomotor (skills). Their explanation for this was that they had little experience teaching manual skills at the college level.

## Table 2-1. Bloom's Taxonomy

| Behavioral Levels | Skills | Examples |
|---|---|---|
| Knowledge | Define, list, name, call, and repeat knowledge or information | Can name six levels of Bloom's taxonomy |
| | Translate, describe, and explain information in one's own words | Can compare and explain Bloom's six levels |
| Application | Apply, demonstrate, and use knowledge in new situations | Can apply Bloom's theory to write learning objectives |
| Analysis | Analyze, compare, question, and break knowledge into parts | Can compare and contrast aspects of Bloom's model |
| Synthesis | Arrange, create, plan, and prepare a new whole from parts | Can design a new learning model |

So how does Bloom's taxonomy, the hierarchy of learning outcomes, relate to writing objectives? Because learning objectives are written to specify the performance (knowledge or skill) that is desired after learning. The taxonomy indicates exactly the behavioral level the learner will know or be able to do at the end of the training experience, for example, "will be able to apply" not just "name."

## Objective Domains

Closely related to Bloom's taxonomy are objective domains, which are categories of objectives that help instructional designers determine several important design elements. These domains—which primarily enable instructional designers to structure objectives, evaluations, and delivery systems—classify the objective of the learning into one of three general categories:

- *cognitive:* skills and knowledge relating to intellectual activity (for example, a learner should be able to know how to repair the equipment)

- *affective:* attitudes, feelings, and values (for example, a learner should be able to offer strategies to overcome negative feelings about repairing certain models)

- *psychomotor:* skills related to physical activity (for example, a learner should be able to physically remove cases and insert boards and should be able to perform other skills requiring the use of the body).

Designers never mix objectives and evaluation tasks that fall within different objective domains because instructional integrity may fail. Inconsistent or inappropriate use of domains can cause dissonance in learners and threaten the success of any program. An illustration of this principle would be using an objective written for one domain and an evaluation task written for another domain. An example might be having an objective that requires a learner to successfully operate a piece of equipment and an evaluation task that asks for an explanation of the theory of operation. The inconsistency in domain can cause confusion as to what the goal of the learning is and cause learners to become discouraged because they were trained for one domain and tested in another.

## Criteria for Writing Objectives

Designers frame objectives based on the perspective of the learner, not the facilitator. Objectives are written at the level of the individual learner and are necessary for each learning activity. Every concept, skill, or objective-worthy behavior should be identified with an objective.

Objectives should be measurable and observable. An objective that cannot be measured or observed is probably not going to have much chance for evaluation. A number of different formats for writing objectives exist. The most recognized format uses four building blocks:

1. ***Audience:*** Although this might appear to be the most independent of the objective elements—the audience is critical to writing them. Designers must validate the audience for each objective. The description should be specific by using the course title or another characteristic (for example, learner in "Handling Stress on the Job").

2. ***Behavior:*** This is the culmination of all the analysis and the purpose for evaluation. This should be a vivid description about an anticipated outcome. Most behavior statements are worded in the format "should be able to" or "will be able to." Be careful about the format selected because "will" and "should" have two distinctly different meanings, and the difference is more than just stylistic. Promising that a learner will be able to do something is different from stating that one should be able to do something. The argument against using "will" is based on the concept of promising absolute results. Behavior statements must not use verbs such as "learn" and "understand" because there is no way to measure or observe them. Verbs such as "create," "list," "construct," and "repair" are observable, measurable, and suitable for statements of behavior in written objectives.

3. ***Condition:*** Objectives in the earlier examples begin with the word "given." Objectives need to state the given to ensure that learners have a complete and consistent foundation from which to work. The condition statement in an objective clearly delineates the conditions for a given behavior. Conditions may include tangible things, such as tools, books, equipment, or hardware. For example, a condition

might say "given a screwdriver and 10 screws" or "provided with a 1329A test set."

4. ***Degree:*** Indicates what it takes to meet an objective. The purpose of learning is to meet an objective. A learner should be able to score some points even if he or she does not hit the mark. As instructional designers write their objectives, they need to be clear about how close to the mark a learner must get to meet them. The difficulty in writing degree statements is the process of realistically setting the degree threshold. Some examples of degree statements include "successfully three times" and "without error."

When objectives are written in this format, they are cleverly called A-B-C-D objectives. These four components are used to clearly and succinctly describe the learning environment and the desired outcome for terminal or enabling objectives. Several reasons exist for this philosophy, but the most persuasive is that, without objectives, there is nothing to evaluate—objectives provide all the building blocks for gauging success. Until the designer defines success (in this case with objectives), the learners can never hope to achieve it.

An example of a four-part objective might be

*Given a complete copy of the* Infoline *on ISD, the Introduction to ISD participant (UMBC course number EDUC 602) should be able to accurately describe the four components of an objective without error when given at least three opportunities to do so.*

The four components of this objective are

1. ***audience:*** the introduction to ISD learner (UMBC course number EDUC 602)

2. ***behavior:*** the ability to accurately describe the four components of an objective

3. ***condition:*** the access to a complete copy of the *Infoline* on ISD

4. ***degree:*** the three opportunities to describe the four components without error.

## Instructional Strategies and Media

Instructional strategies, or methods, are techniques that designers use to link objectives with learners. Lectures, group discussions, and case studies all serve as the link between the learner and the subject matter.

When objectives have been refined and tests have been designed to validate learning, the designer considers instructional strategies, or how to structure the content. To make this and other strategic decisions, Nadler (1994) has noted that the "designer must know enough about learning theory to know what has been researched and theorized in the past. Although there are proponents and opponents for every learning theory . . . the designer may not want to choose sides, but at times must make decisions as to which learning theory is most appropriate for a specific learning experience."

Training theorists and practitioners often advocate using strategies related to experiential, active, or discovery learning. This means that learners participate in activities—such as role play, discussion, and hands-on practice—that help them discover what to do for good job performance. In contrast, didactic strategies involve telling or showing learners what to do.

Active learning tends to be more meaningful and memorable than passive learning, but it isn't always appropriate or feasible. If there truly is only one right way to perform a task, learners may well resent spending time discovering it while a knowing trainer withholds the answer. If time for learning is short or unskilled performance is dangerous, it's best to tell or show learners what to do.

As mentioned earlier, in the early 1970s, Knowles coined the term ***andragogy*** to describe principles of adult learning and teaching (as distinguished from ***pedagogy***, a term applied to children). Many now believe that the facilitative or participatory training style—in which the trainer guides the learner to discover what he or she needs to learn—is more appropriate for adult learners. This trainer-facilitated and learner-centered environment better suits adult learning requirements.

Still, the traditional, instructive style does have its place in certain situations. The trick is to intuitively understand when to apply the appropriate method. When designers become aware of the differences in learning and teaching styles, they can consciously apply the correct method for the learner and the situation.

At this point, the designer must select the instructional strategy to facilitate learning. Instructional strategies, sometimes called ***presentation strategies***, are the mechanisms through which instruction in presented. The most common strategies include lecture, role play, group discussion, self-discovery, self-paced instruction, case studies, and games. See Chapter 3, "An Exploration of Instructional Methods," for more details regarding selecting instructional strategies. The appropriate strategy to use for a presentation depends on a variety of factors, including

- type of learning (verbal information, intellectual skills, cognitive strategy, attitude, or motor skills)
- audience
- demographics or profile
- number of learners
- media
- budget
- physical site (centralized, decentralized, or specialized).

Each factor, in combination with others, influences the choice of strategy for presenting, reinforcing, and assessing the retention of the material.

As mentioned previously, course design is linked to course development through a series of documents used to create an initial blueprint. The blueprint should list the course objectives. Supportive information about the subject matter or course content should be linked to each objective.

Training and content experts together select the instructional content. They systematically define the critical content components or modules and show how the instructional strategies will be used to introduce content. In addition, they determine appropriate learning techniques, develop opportunities for practice, and select appropriate media. All media should have a definite purpose: Designers must choose them to amplify learning, not to entertain a bored audience.

The instructional specification includes

- module name
- introduction (content summary, utility, importance)
- sequence of topics and activities (flow, transitions, links).

For each objective, documentation should elaborate

- special teaching points
- instructional methods to be used
- media requirements
- testing requirements.

## Principles and Types of Sequencing Content

During the analysis phase, instructional designers identify certain types of relationships among job tasks. Some tasks are subordinate to others, some are equal in importance but must be performed in a particular sequence, some tasks have a logical relationship but may be performed in any order, and some tasks within a job are unrelated to others.

During the design phase, learning objectives are often arranged into a logical learning sequence. Sequencing and structuring are very closely related. A *sequence* is the order in which information or skills are taught, whereas *structure* refers to the relationships among skills and topics. Structure is important because it provides a framework for learning; structured information aids in learning more quickly and allows learners to remember what they have learned more efficiently.

Typically, instruction is sequenced according to tasks, topics, or problems. For example, a new salesperson's training might follow a task chronology (greet customer; determine needs; if appropriate, present merchandise and suggest accessories; close and record transaction; thank customer and invite him or her to visit store again). Or, such training might group tasks by topics (customer service; demonstration and description of merchandise; mechanics of recording sales, returns, and other transactions).

The problem-solving approach is similar to the topic approach but emphasizes problem diagnosis and solution. This might be appropriate for a mid-level sales training workshop (determining customer priorities efficiently, handling difficult customers tactfully, completing complex transactions accurately).

Within a framework of tasks, topics, and problem solving, instruction is usually either sequenced step-by-step in job performance order, in order of priority or frequency of performance, or in these orders:

- chronological
- topical
- procedural (step-by-step)
- problem and solution
- general to specific
- simple to complex
- overview, demonstration, practice
- known to unknown or unknown to known
- less risky to more risky.

At this point, the instructional designer selects the overall training strategies. Details can be worked out when specific materials are chosen. For now, the designer makes general decisions about the training method or methods and the training media. Some questions to ask include "Will the course include on-the-job training, classroom instruction, lab or workshop instruction, or self-instruction?" and "Will the course use textbooks, consumable workbooks, computers, interactive videodisks, or audiotapes and videotapes?"

The selected strategies must match the stated objectives of the course. For example, the strategies for a course to help trainees master computer skills should not rely on pencil-and-paper activities. Participants will need opportunities for hands-on computer practice to pass a job-related evaluation at the course's end.

Having completed the analysis, written the objectives, and designed test items, the designer now has a good idea of what is going to be included in the training program. The next step is to outline the information and develop a course map, which identifies all the steps that lead to completion of the course. Some designers develop the course map as soon as they have completed the job and task analysis, whereas others wait until they have begun to develop the course materials and instructional strategies. Either way, it is critical to keep the audience and the purpose of the course in mind while the designer develops it.

## Course Maps

A course map lists in hierarchical order the modules within units. Some trainers describe the hierarchy as modules within chapters or as units within lessons within modules. The terminology is not important. Figure 2-6 shows an example of a course map.

# Figure 2-6. Example of a Course Map

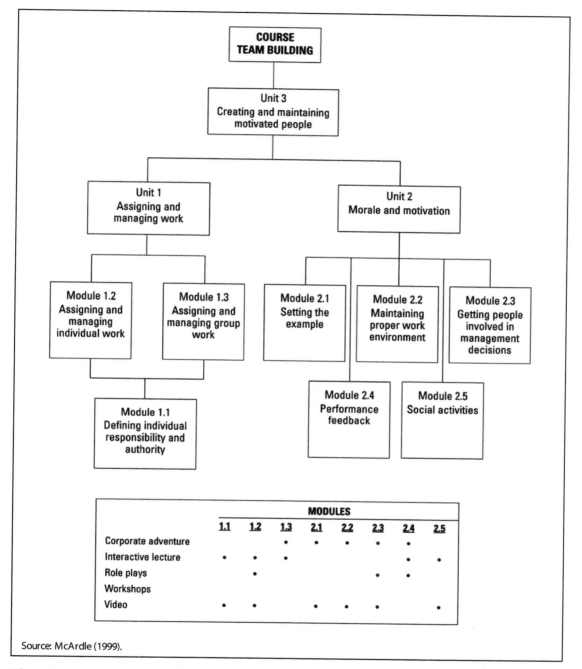

Source: McArdle (1999).

This map is accompanied by media selections and support requirements. The designer should think about the following influences on the course as he or she designs the course map to ensure that the design is consistent with them:

- course objectives
- class size
- training site

- pre- and postcourse work

- course materials

- delivery strategy and instructor needs

- multilevel audience experience

- course relationship to job conditions

- learner motivation and accountability.

Instructional designers need to consider the big picture when they develop a course or program. Once they have identified the reason for the course, the next step is to develop a course program or program sequence. Here are some guidelines for sequencing an entire course:

- Focus on what happens on the job.

- Use the job analysis to establish the sequence of chapters.

- Arrange the course in sequence, from general to specific, from simple to complex.

- When sequencing has no job-related basis, arrange the course in the most logical fashion for the learner.

- If a module for performance is available, such as a problem-solving or a training design model, use it as a guide for sequencing.

- Use the same delivery advisory group to test the sequence that validated other areas of the analysis and design process.

## Modules

Adult learners respond best to small, organized units of learning, so designers should organize the course content into modules. A ***module*** (sometimes called a ***lesson***) is the smallest unit of learning and provides content and practice on the basis of predefined learning objectives. Each module relates to a specific task in the task analysis so that at the end of the training, the learner should be able to perform the task.

### Sample Course and Module Design

The following example of course and module design illustrates a course in problem analysis that was put together by Rosemary Brehm. At this point, objectives, test items, and topic content have been created. The next step is to develop a course and module map. The first thing to do, according to McArdle (1999), is list all the elements that are necessary to teach. Next, the designer organizes them in a logical framework and then develops subtopics.

Here's an example of a course and module design for a program:

*Chapter 1: Problem Analysis*

> *Module 1: How to state the problem*
>
> *Module 2: How to define the standard*
>
> *Module 3: How to define the difference*
>
> *Chapter 2: Cause Identification*
>
> *Module 1: How to determine training deficiencies*
>
> *Module 2: How to determine other deficiencies*
>
> *Chapter 3: Data Collection*
>
> *Module 1: How to create data-collection questions*
>
> *Module 2: How to use data-collection sources*
>
> *Module 3: How to manage data collection*
>
> *Chapter 4: Idea Generation*
>
> *Module 1: How to use individual techniques*
>
> *Module 2: How to use group techniques*
>
> *Chapter 5: Solution Selection*
>
> *Module 1: How to evaluate ideas*
>
> *Module 2: How to use group techniques*

Each learning module contains

- objectives

- knowledge content to enable the learner to complete the task

- task content

- practice activities to help reach the objectives

- an assessment mechanism, such as a test item, to determine whether the objectives were achieved.

Other factors to take into account when creating the module include

- the best method to use to get objectives across

- timing and breaks

- the amount of material to cover

- class or group size for activities

- simulation of job conditions.

The module design serves as a major section of the course blueprint for developing the content and instructional strategies. Each module should contain

- an objective statement

- identification of the content topics

- identification of trainer and learner activities that will result in mastery of the objective, including methods and media used by the trainer and the learner.

## The Design Report

The design report is a summary of the analysis and design completed to date. It serves as the preliminary communication to inform training sponsors of progress to date and provides an opportunity for suggestions and feedback. The report is a way to ensure that training meets sponsor expectations because their support for training objectives and course outcomes is critical to the success of the designer as well as the success of the program and the trainees.

The report serves to inform sponsors of the proposed training, it provides a roadmap for the instructional designer to use in developing the training, and it provides the course instructor with background information regarding how and why the training was developed.

A design report contains several narrative components:

- purpose of the course
- summary of the analysis
- scope of the course
- test item strategy
- course and module design
- delivery strategy
- level of evaluation to be tested.

## Lesson Plans

After completing the course and module design, the next step involves developing a lesson, or session, plan. A lesson plan allows the learning professional to determine in advance whether the delivery sequence is correct, the content is relevant to the topic and the learner, and the instructional strategies are appropriate. The lesson plan also acts as a resource checklist. It allows the WLP professional to prepare for any information or material that may be required for the lesson, such as handouts, overheads, videotapes, flipcharts, and wall charts.

### Lesson Plan Format

The set of detailed notes that make up the lesson plan will guide the designer and the facilitator through the material development and delivery processes. The elements of a lesson should include

- session title

## Table 2-2. Format of a Lesson Plan

| Timing | Content (What to Be Taught) | Training Techniques | Trainee Activity | Training Aids |
|---|---|---|---|---|
| | | | | |

- learning objectives
- timing
- key learning points
- brief content synopsis
- presentation methodology
- definition of terms
- key questions to ask
- resource requirements
- learner activities
- topic transitions
- review checks
- learner issues.

One format, suggested by McArdle (1999) and shown in Table 2-2, includes five columns: timing, content, training techniques, trainee activity, and training aids.

Following is a description of each column:

- **Timing:** This column lists the time to spend on each topic and subtopic of each session. A typical training day includes approximately 55 minutes in an hour for training. The facilitator should provide at least 10 percent of the time to introduce or make a transition to the topic and devote 70 percent of the time to content delivery, which might include preparing the learner to learn (stating the objective), presenting the material, and practicing the material with an exercise and feedback. The final 20 percent of the time should be devoted to summary, conclusion, and transition to the next lesson or module.

- *Content:* This column lists the topic and subtopics to cover during each session. Training professionals should not combine sessions, but develop and deliver each session topic independently, using transition statements to bridge from one topic or subtopic to another. In the session plan, the facilitator indicates introductions, breaks, and sequences for each session. Facilitators should avoid "run-on" sessions without using transition statements. (Run-on sessions are sessions that continue after lunch or another break or even from one day to the next.) Content delivery should take the form of complete and inclusive parts.

- *Training techniques:* This column explains in basic terms whether the session is to be, for example, discovery learning.

- *Trainee activity:* This column lists the types of things that the learner will be doing during the session (listening, looking, practicing, and so forth). By documenting this information, the training professional will have the opportunity to build a variety of activities into his or her training course in advance.

- *Training aids:* This column lists the instructional aids and strategies or peripherals that the facilitator will use and the order in which he or she will use them.

As the facilitator begins to write the plan, he or she should consider two questions: What is the purpose of this training presentation? What do learners need to know?

## Designers and Facilitators: Who Does What?

The training designer and the instructor, or facilitator, often play different roles in lesson design and development. However, the same person often designs and presents a training program. This is especially true in organizations with small training departments.

Knowing who is responsible for certain decisions in the ISD process is important. In lesson design and development, the designer outlines the lesson, suggests approaches to topics, determines instructional periods and breaks, and selects and prepares major instructional material, such as tests and guides.

The following list shows how responsibility may be divided between the designer and facilitator in lesson design and development.

### General Division of Responsibility

The lesson designer

- chooses major strategies and training aids

- designates number of instructional periods and break points

- selects and prepares participant handouts, such as exercise sheets, data sheets, and instructor and learner guides

- selects principal components of content and evaluation.

The instructor or facilitator

- selects details of strategies and implements presentation

- implements use of major training aids and chooses and implements use of minor training aids

- selects and implements structure and timing with instructional periods

- implements use of materials—detailed selections and timing

- selects and implements ways to stimulate interest, motivate, and present material.Lesson Content Organization

Too much information at one time creates confusion. **Chunking** is a term for breaking down concepts into meaningful parts. The learning professional should give the learner a maximum of three large pieces of information at a time. In a session, if the topic has three major components, the facilitator should deliver them within an hour. After delivering the three large chunks within an hour, it's time to summarize and break.

The designer should cluster the topic information into organized sections, such as introduction, body, and activities. Next, he or she should use the technique of "grading the content" to determine the appropriate amount of information to deliver. Figure 2-7 shows a simple way of grading, or targeting, the material to deliver.

## Figure 2-7. Technique to Help Grade Content

The **must-know** information is the enabling knowledge that the learner needs to know to perform the task or job. The **need-to-know** information may be needed for the learner to gain a clear understanding of the essential information presented during the session. The **nice-to-know** information encompasses items that are not necessary to know and might illustrate the points covered in the session.

Assuming the designer develops instruction that targets the bull's-eye, the must-know area,

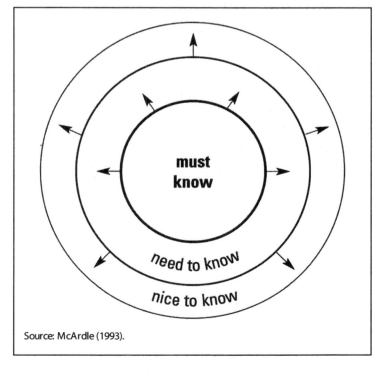

Source: McArdle (1993).

a certain amount of time also would be spent in the need-to-know area as a review. If time permits, facilitators can let the learners look at the nice-to-know area; however, the time would probably be better spent reviewing the need-to-know and must-know areas. It is better to deliver too little well than to deliver too much badly.

## Course Description

Putting together a course description is like doing a crossword puzzle: Some parts are easy to fill in, some are difficult, and later information may invalidate earlier choices. The final course description should explain the why, who, what, how, when, and where of the course:

- *Why* the course is needed includes the course objectives and the expected benefits—for the organization, learners and their supervisors, colleagues, and organizational clients or customers—and the estimated dollar value of these benefits.

- *Who* (job titles or number of people) explains who is involved in the course's analysis, design, development, implementation, and evaluation. The who includes

  - who is to receive training

  - prerequisites of entry requirements, if any

  - availability of learners for training

  - whether trainers will be working with SMEs, facilitators, other trainers, training managers, consultants, suppliers, or other individuals

  - staff trainers' special interests, knowledge, and skills

  - availability of people involved in designing, developing, implementing, and evaluating the course.

- *What* aspects of the course development team's work must be coordinated and describes who will oversee the coordination. This should include

  - general course content—major topics, tasks, and task clusters

  - KSAs to be learned or improved

  - approximate proportions of cognitive learning (knowledge), psychomotor learning (skill), and affective learning (attitude) the course will involve

  - how topics, tasks, and KSAs have been identified and analyzed and their relevance to improved job performance

  - how a participant demonstrates successful learning (for example, pencil-and-paper tasks, oral presentations, construction of a model, performance of an activity).

- *How* course content is sequenced and what strategies are employed to engage participants in learning includes

- learning events and activities

- whether learning will be accomplished in a group or individually

- which portions of the course, if any, will be designed for self-instruction

- whether portions of the course allow a trainer or participant to choose among alternative activities.

- **When** the course will take place and how it will be run includes

  - whether it will be run once, several times, or many times, and whether it will be on company time or on learners' time

  - whether it must be run in a particular season, on particular days, or at particular times

  - expected course completion date

  - whether everyone will participate at the same time or at different times, according to such factors as available sites or organizational levels

  - whether the course will run in segments or as a whole

  - whether any pilot tests will take place and, if so, whether alternative designs will be offered.

- **Where** the course will be conducted. This should include

  - whether it will be at a central site, such as a corporate training center or at individual plants, offices, field sites, or any combination thereof

  - special facilities requirements—electrical power, lighting, space, seating, and viewing arrangements

  - if all or part of the course is self-instruction, whether learners will perform this training at their regular workstations, at learning centers stocked with special equipment, or at home.

---

## Example of a Course Description

25 Tips for Communicating Online

Length: 1 day

**Prerequisites:** Learners should be able to develop user's guides and other printed material for user support. The material is presented in Technical Communication 101.

**About this seminar:** 25 Tips for Communicating Online explores how to adapt writing skills honed for the printed page to the screen. Learn how to overcome the limitations of reading online through effective organization and tight writing. Specifically, learn

- techniques for structuring information online

## Example of a Course Description, continued

- issues in screen design and navigation online
- ways to engage readers through visual variety and interaction
- tight writing techniques
- tips for bringing readers to online content.

Through hands-on exercises, you will practice the techniques presented in class.

*Who should attend:* Technical communicators, business communicators, and trainers who are experienced in writing for the page or developing material for the classroom and want to reorient their skills for the computer screen. Experienced online communicators and web-based training developers might find this workshop a good refresher (and may pick up a few new ideas, too).

What you will learn:

*Terminal objective:* Adapt strategies for presenting content from the page or classroom to the screen.

*Enabling objectives:* To achieve the objective, you should be able to

1. Name the four fundamental ways that communicating online differs from communicating on the page or in the classroom.
2. Describe at least three ways that online learning content differs from content in other media.
3. Explain how to help users navigate through online content.
4. Explain how to effectively use typography online.
5. Explain how to place content on the screen for maximum effect.
6. Describe at least three techniques for communicating interactively online.
7. Describe at least three techniques for communicating visually online.
8. Describe at least three techniques for writing online material.
9. State the role of tools in producing online content.
10. Describe at least two issues to consider when maintaining online content.

The design team will also need to determine how much the course is expected to cost. This includes such factors as how the course will be funded, such as through an organization-wide budget category or a training department budget, by charging departments of workers that use the course, through grants from outside sources, by the participants, or through some combination of sources.

## Outputs of Design

Various documents record decisions made during the design phase and note steps and decisions yet to be made in the development phase. A course design should consist of the following:

- *A budget request:* Unless the course's funding is already set, a budget needs to be requested. If only the total budget allocation is known, the design should still specify funding categories (personnel, equipment and supplies, and facilities). Some organizations demand budget justification. This can provide an opportunity to justify, for example, using a conference center with the necessary equipment and supplies versus a less-expensive site that involves extra company time and expense to lease and ship equipment.

- *A list of course objectives:* A sequenced list of objectives should be prepared, along with any corresponding test items.

- *A course description:* A course description should record broad design considerations and decisions and support a budget request (if made). A course description will vary in length, depending on organizational custom and the scope of the course.

- *A project or administrative plan:* A project or an administrative plan should specify individual responsibilities and deadlines for course development.

- *A list of needed equipment:* A tentative list should be made of needed equipment, materials, and supplies. A final list will emerge with completed lesson and learning plans.

# Basics of Course Development

*Development* is the process of creating, testing, and producing usable instructional materials. In the design phase, the learning professional defined the topic to be developed by creating learning objectives and establishing topic content.

Throughout the development process, training team members—the people who are knowledgeable in the content area, instructional design, and evaluation that the designer has selected to work with him or her—continually review the major training materials in development. They review the revisions and use pilot testing to check program material prior to delivery of the formal training program.

Development should proceed according to some project planning and control method. The course director will need a record of who has responsibility for course development steps and will need to coordinate and monitor intermediate due dates to ensure that the course is ready on time.

## Training Materials

During the development phase, media and materials will be located, selected, or created. Off-the-shelf materials can be used as is or adapted when appropriate. For example, a film may contain an excellent illustration of a procedure, but uses many terms that don't fit the organizational climate. In this case, the design team may determine that the facilitator should run the film with the sound shut off and read a script aloud. Or, they may determine that the trainer could give a special explanation of the film prior to viewing.

Training materials to be gathered, created, or designed include

- instructional guides, such as lesson and learning plans, that detail introductory material

- transitions that lead from one instructional activity to another

- integrators that tie course activities together and link them to participants' prior learning

- administrative aids, such as participant rosters; maps; material, equipment, or supplies checklists; and name tags

- evaluation materials (see the next section)

- participant guides, such as texts, workbooks, and job aids

- activity aids, such as checklists, role-play scripts, case studies, and lab exercises

- actual equipment and supplies—paper, videotapes and videotape players, films, projectors, computers, charts, pointers, flipcharts, markers, spare parts, and so forth.

## Evaluation Materials

Evaluation can be either formative or summative and must be tied to objectives. Formative evaluation occurs continually throughout the analysis, design, development, and implementation phases. Summative evaluation occurs only after course completion.

Although, as baseball great Yogi Berra said, "you can observe a lot by watching," subjective impressions should be only part of evaluation. A plan for objective measures of success and written materials devised during the development phase should support both formative and summative evaluation.

A formative evaluation plan describes means for improving a course and for assessing learners' in-training progress and attitudes toward training. A summative evaluation plan describes such measures as posttraining employee performance, turnover, and customer comments. An overall evaluation plan should tell how and when, throughout the entire ISD process, information will be distributed and collected, and from and by whom.

Many instructional designers conduct one or more pilot tests of a course before carrying it out on a large scale. If a control group is used, or if more than one pilot test is conducted, designers may test alternative designs. But this is a luxury that many organizations cannot afford.

Evaluation techniques should cause as little disruption as possible. Designers should prepare forms that are clearly worded and quick and easy to fill out. Evaluation results can lead to design refinements by answering questions about these training components:

- **Tasks:** Do instructors or learners believe that tasks are sequenced properly for effective, efficient learning? Do they believe learning has been broken down into tasks that are not boringly easy or overwhelmingly difficult?

- **Topics:** Do instructors or learners think any information is missing? Do they find any information to be misleading or wrong?

- **Learning activities and materials:** Do learners feel they get enough feedback and practice? Do they and their supervisors consider the course useful? Do they consider it interesting, difficult, or fun? Do learners and facilitators consider learning activities and materials worth the time (and money) invested in them?

- **Tests:** Do tests call for participants to demonstrate (rather than describe) learning? Do participants consider tests fair? Do participants and their supervisors consider tests reasonable indicators of ability to perform on the job?

- **Productivity:** Have measures (absenteeism, turnover, rework, and speed and quality tests) improved for individuals or groups since their training?

## Training Documentation Materials

During course development, the design team should create a documentation plan that tells what training records will be kept, how, by whom, and for how long. Training records may be kept on paper, on file cards, on microfilm, or in computer files. Original or backup records may be maintained in the training, information systems, planning, or legal department.

Original training records or copies may need to be forwarded to a government agency, a private regulatory group, or a professional agency that issues credentials. Record retention and destruction schedules may be established by law, organizational policy, or designers' recommendation.

During development, the design team must develop or copy any needed documentation materials. For example, the training department probably has a standard daily attendance form that needs only to be copied. But a new, legally mandated safety course might require a form documenting employees' attendance according to specific units within the course.

Organizations typically save a course history that shows who was responsible for various aspects of ISD; samples of forms; the course design document and lesson and learning plans; the course budget; attendance by learners, trainers, facilitators, and guests; and evaluation records about individual participants, instructor performance, and course effectiveness and efficiency.

## Development Outputs

The outcome of the development stage is a training program that is ready to be implemented. The development process consists of five phases, each one of which leads to the next, as shown in Table 2-3.

## Table 2-3. Development Outputs

| Phase | Outputs |
|---|---|
| 1 | Develop the following:<br>• training program content<br>• graphics and media needs<br>• lesson plans<br>• instructor guides<br>• evaluation needs<br>• software needs<br>• review of the materials developed. |
| 2 | Revise the following:<br>• training program content<br>• graphics and media needs<br>• lesson plans<br>• instructor guides<br>• evaluation needs<br>• software needs<br>• review of the revised material. |
| 3 | Do the following:<br>• conduct the test<br>• revise the program on the basis of the test<br>• schedule a second test if needed. |
| 4 | Do the following:<br>• pilot test a prototype program<br>• evaluate the pilot test<br>• identify the required revisions<br>• revise the program as required (on the basis of the pilot test)<br>• schedule a second test, if needed. |
| 5 | Do the following:<br>• finalize the training program content<br>• produce the training program in final form. |

# ✓ Chapter 2 Knowledge Check

**1. What does ADDIE stand for?**

__ A. Assess, design, develop, implement, evaluate

__ B. Assess, discover, design, implement, evaluate

__ C. Analyze, design, develop, implement, evaluate

__ D. Analyze, discover, develop, implement, evaluate

**2. Which of the following best describes the key benefit of Gagne's nine instructional events?**

__ A. This theory is a collection of strategies to quickly produce instructional packages depending on types of tradeoffs between design and delivery.

__ B. This theory supports the notion of lesson plan design and an ideal teaching sequence that enhances retention because training is based on the way that learners process information.

__ C. This theory outlines a learner-centered instructional style that guides the learner to discover what he or she needs to learn.

__ D. This theory outlines six behavioral levels including knowledge, comprehension, application, analysis, synthesis, and evaluation.

**3. Which of the following instructional design models is based on the assumption that design happens in a context of project management where a project plan establishes roles, tasks, timelines, budgets, checkpoints, and supervisory procedures?**

__ A. Rapid instructional design

__ B. Dick and Carey systems approach for instructional design

__ C. Seels and Glasgow instructional system design model

__ D. Smith and Ragan instructional system design model

**4. Which of the following instructional design models states that a designer goes through a three-stage process: analysis, strategy development, and evaluation?**

__ A. Rapid instructional design

__ B. Dick and Carey systems approach for instructional design

__ C. Seels and Glasgow instructional system design model

__ D. Smith and Ragan systematic instructional design model

5. **Accelerated learning is a learning strategy that involves both the right and left hemispheres and the cortex and limbic systems of the brain, thus making learning more natural. Which of the following is *not* a characteristic of a learning environment that is conducive to accelerated learning?**

___ A.  Provides learning challenges for learners to overcome

___ B.  Supports both learners and trainers

___ C.  Presents material both visually and verbally

___ D.  Provides for group-based learning

6. **Sequencing of instruction is important to its effectiveness. Which of the following is *not* a type of sequencing?**

___ A.  Procedural order

___ B.  Chronological order

___ C.  Problem and solution

___ D.  Performance/skill

7. **A client wants a designer to develop a training class to improve declining sales of the salesforce. What is the best thing to do first?**

___ A.  Locate historical documentation.

___ B.  Perform a front-end analysis.

___ C.  Confirm the budget and timeframe.

___ D.  Identify representatives with top sales.

8. **Which of the following is a principle of human performance improvement?**

___ A.  Lesson plans are an integral component of most instructional design projects with a sequential set of events that lead to a desired performance goal.

___ B.  Training may not be the appropriate solution, and a needs analysis should be conducted to ensure that the performance gap can be remedied by training.

___ C.  Selection of an appropriate instructional design method depends on types of tradeoffs between design and delivery of instruction to achieve the performance goal.

___ D.  Bloom's taxonomy defines six behavioral levels and specifically defines the desired performance goal.

9. **Who is credited with the idea that a learning objective should contain a condition statement, a performance statement, and a criterion statement?**

    __ A.   Malcolm Knowles

    __ B.   Robert Gagne

    __ C.   Benjamin Bloom

    __ D.   Robert Mager

10. **Which of the following is described as a collection of strategies for quickly producing instructional packages that enable learners to achieve a set of specific learning objectives? This model involves alternatives, enhancements, and modifications to the ADDIE model in the form of tradeoffs between design and delivery.**

    __ A.   Rapid instructional design

    __ B.   Dick and Carey systems approach for instructional design

    __ C.   Seels and Glasgow instructional system design model

    __ D.   Smith and Ragan instructional system design model

11. **Which of the following best describes Bloom's taxonomy and its relevance to writing objectives?**

    __ A.   The taxonomy proposes specific and measurable performance objectives with three components: behavior, condition, and standard.

    __ B.   The taxonomy states that learning goals and objectives are the same and should be written using the A-B-C-D format.

    __ C.   Because learning objectives are written to specify the performance (knowledge and skill) that is desired after the learning, the taxonomy specifies exactly what the learner will know or be able to do at the end of the training experience.

    __ D.   The taxonomy proposes that behavior should be specific and observable.

12. **Which of the following objective domains—categories of objectives used to determine design elements—focuses on the skills and knowledge relating to intellectual activity such as knowing how to edit a manuscript?**

    __ A.   Cognitive

    __ B.   Interactive

    __ C.   Psychomotor

    __ D.   Affective

13. **Instruction on how to operate a forklift is most likely to have which type of objective?**

    \_\_ A.  Affective

    \_\_ B.  Psychomotor

    \_\_ C.  Application

    \_\_ D.  Knowledge

# References

Biech, E. (2005). *Training for Dummies®*. Hoboken, NJ: Wiley Publishing.

Butruille, S.G. (1989). "Lesson Design and Development." *Infoline* No. 258906.

Carliner, S. (2002). *Designing E-Learning*. Alexandria, VA: ASTD Press.

———. (2003). *Training Design Basics*. Alexandria, VA: ASTD Press.

Dick, W.O., and L. Carey. (1996). *The Systematic Design of Instruction*. 3rd edition. New York: HarperCollins College.

Dick, W.O., L. Carey, and J.O. Carey. (2004). *The Systematic Design of Instruction*. 6th edition. Boston: Allyn & Bacon.

Fairbanks, D.M. (1992). "Accelerated Learning." *Infoline* No. 259209.

Gagne, R.M., L.J. Briggs, and W.W. Wager. (1988). *Principles of Instructional Design*. 3rd edition. New York: Holt, Rinehart, and Winston.

Hodell, C. (1997). "Basics of Instructional Systems Development." *Infoline* No. 259706.

———. (2000). *ISD From the Ground Up*. Alexandria, VA: ASTD Press.

Kirkpatrick, D.L. (1994). *Evaluating Training Programs*. San Francisco: Berrett-Koehler.

Knowles, M. (1984). *The Adult Learner: A Neglected Species*. 3rd edition. Gulf Publishing Company: Houston, TX.

Mager, R.F. (1962). *Preparing Objectives for Programmed Instruction*. Palo Alto, CA: Fearon.

McArdle, G.E. (1993). *Delivering Effective Training Sessions*. Menlo Park, CA: Crisp Publications.

———. (1999). *Training Design and Delivery*. Alexandria, VA: ASTD Press.

Nadler, L. (1994). *Designing Training Programs*. 2nd edition. Houston, TX: Gulf Publishing.

Russo, C., and J. Mitchell, eds. (2005). "The *Infoline* Dictionary of Basic Trainer Terms." *Infoline* No. 250513.

Sanders, E.S., and S. Thiagarajan. (2005). *Performance Intervention Maps: 39 Strategies for Solving Your Organization's Problems*. Alexandria, VA: ASTD Press.

Seels, B., and R. Glasgow. (1998). *Making Instructional Design Decisions*. Upper Saddle River, NJ: Prentice-Hall.

Senge, P. (1990). *The Fifth Discipline*. New York: Currency.

Sharpe, C. (1997). "Course Design and Development." *Infoline* No. 258905.

Smith, P.L., and T.J. Ragan. (2004). *Instructional Design*. 3rd edition. Hoboken, NJ: Wiley/Jossey-Bass.

Thiagarajan, S. (2000). "Rapid Instructional Development." In G. Piskurich, P. Beckschi, and B. Hall, eds., *The ASTD Handbook of Training Design and Delivery*. New York: McGraw-Hill.

Treacy, M., and F. Wiersema. (1995). *The Discipline of Market Leaders: Choose Your Customers, Narrow Your Focus, Dominate Your Market*. New York: Perseus Books.

# 3
# Instructional Methods

Instructional methods are techniques that designers use to link objectives with learners. Lectures, group discussions, and case studies all serve as links between the learner and subject matter, much the same way as a book or webpage connects the user to information. Distribution methods are the ways designers deliver instructional methods. Proper matching of distribution and instructional methods and platforms saves time and energy for both the designer and the learner.

When creating effective learning, a WLP professional must consider the array of instructional methods available. Time, distance, budget, and coordination of schedules are only some of the issues to be considered while designing the most appropriate format for learning. Choosing instructional strategies that meet participants' needs and create an atmosphere conducive to learning is important.

Instructional designers need to determine the distribution methods and instructional methods they will be working with early in their planning. These two elements must be in place before designers get too involved with the design process.

Instructional designers make choices that determine how their learners interact with the subject matter. The designer's tool of matching innovative distribution methods and instructional methods is important.

## Learning Objectives:

☑ Describe various factors to consider prior to selecting instructional strategies.

☑ Define active training and list three techniques.

☑ Describe e-learning techniques including simulations, feedback, and navigation best practices.

# Instructional Strategies

What is meant by instruction, and what is meant by instructional strategies? The central purpose of any training or education program is to promote learning. Instruction promotes learning through a set of events developed to initiate, activate, and support learning.

WLP professionals use instructional strategies to

- motivate learners

- help learners prepare for learning

- enable learners to apply and practice learning

- assist learners in retaining and transferring what they have learned

- integrate their own preferences with other skills and knowledge.

Instructional strategies, sometimes called presentation strategies, are the mechanisms through which instruction is presented.

Based on the needs assessment and the learning objectives, the instructional strategy is selected. In some instances, the instructional designer can choose a single strategy for an entire course. This is true when the course is brief and requires only one strategy. At other times, the designer may choose just one strategy because all the material is similar in nature and choosing the same strategy reinforces the relationships among the different units. In still other instances, when the material in each unit is sufficiently different that it benefits from a different approach to presentation, the designer chooses different approaches for different units. Or, he or she might choose different approaches in different units to provide variety for the learners.

Before choosing techniques and training materials, the designer must consider these factors:

- ***Instructional objectives:*** Instructional techniques and activities must match the objectives—whether they involve cognitive learning (knowledge), psychomotor learning (skill), or affective learning (attitude):

  - Cognitive learning involves mental processes and the acquisition of knowledge.

  - Psychomotor skills involve manipulation of objectives or machinery based on mental decisions. Training techniques include demonstration, practice, simulation, and mock-ups.

  - Attitude involves motivation and perceptions. Training activities include role play, discussion, and brainstorming.

- ***Cost or budget:*** Designers must always keep in mind cost benefit when determining training media and activities. Does the effectiveness of the activity in helping learners meet learning objectives justify the expense?

- ***Lesson content:*** Techniques and media must be consistent with the lesson content.

- *Learners' knowledge and expectations:* Learners will come from different ages and backgrounds as well as varying levels of experience and knowledge. Training activities must meet their needs while avoiding the extremes of being overly simple or too complicated. Trainers must consider the learners' level of comfort with different activities.

- *Time availability:* Expected duration of training activities must realistically fit within time constraints.

- *Facilities, equipment, and material:* Even such constraints as fixed row seating can greatly affect the choice of training and learning activities, and the availability of equipment obviously affects the choice of training media.

Each factor, in combination with the others, influences the choice of strategy for presenting, reinforcing, and assessing the retention of the material. A model depicting the relationship among the factors is shown in Figure 3-1.

## Context

Context may be the most important element that can help determine the success of any learning initiative. An in-depth analysis of the context should be the departure point of

## Figure 3-1. Factors Influencing Instructional Strategies

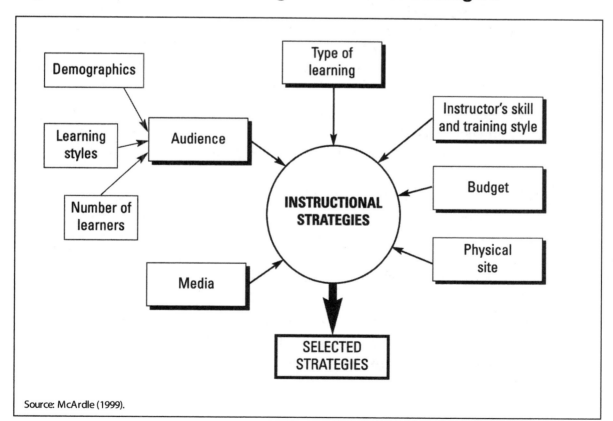

Source: McArdle (1999).

every learning design effort. To consider the context, take into account learner characteristics, including:

- *physical features:* age, gender, disabilities
- *education:* fields of study, degrees earned, computer literacy
- *cultural background:* language, place of origin, traditions, sensitive subjects
- *employment background:* experience, time in current job, relationships with other participants
- *expectations:* reasons for attending the course, expected results.

This information enables designers to consider the following design points:

- *Language to use:* Knowing the audience provides context regarding the requirements for use of and definition of vocabulary—for example, engineers and psychologists require different vocabulary, as do senior citizens and generation Xers. Designers should be wary of using too many technical words, slang, inclusive use of gender (he and she), and unintentionally offending learners with wording.

- *Information to focus on:* Knowing participants' educational background and experience will help to avoid redundancies that could bore learners. It is important to focus on the content required for learners to accomplish the learning objectives.

- *Learner preparation:* Designers must ensure that learners are ready for the instruction. Before beginning the course, learners may need to refresh their communication skills or take a prerequisite course before they can understand the content. In the case of e-learning, they may need to update their computer skills.

- *Course pace:* Designers need to know the motivation and current knowledge of the learners to establish the course rhythm. Going too slow or too fast can bore or overwhelm learners. Gauging the time the participants have available and are willing to allocate to the instruction as well as how soon they expect to acquire skills and knowledge is also important.

- *Use of peer learning:* Learners with previous experience or knowledge can be disruptive or useful, depending on how the facilitation is structured. Identifying veterans and using their knowledge as a resource can be helpful. Experienced participants will most likely be happy to help and to get involved in their peers' training, and should be encouraged to do so.

- *Amount of hand-holding:* Designers must determine the amount and the kind of support that learners will need during the instruction. They need to try to understand the learners' feelings toward the instruction, topics, or skills that may increase anxiety or stress and try to develop a support scheme to ease learner apprehension.

- *Amount and types of interaction:* One factor that makes instruction different than reading a book is interaction. Knowing the learners will help predict their preferred ways to interact, such as communicating by email and phone.

- *Learner attitudes and motivations:* To keep participants motivated, WLP professionals try to understand the participants' reasons for attending the instruction and whether the instruction is mandatory.

- *Expected outcomes:* To satisfy audience needs, their expectations must be assessed. A well-designed course that does not meet learner objectives will not satisfy learner or organizational needs. Designers should verify the organizational and learner needs prior to developing the instruction.

- *Access issues:* It is important to determine the access participants will have to applications and tools they need. In the case of e-learning, areas to assess include hardware, software, bandwidth issues, and communication.

- *Teaching methods:* Teaching methods depend as much on the trainer as on the audience and the contents of the course. Learning requires commitment and participation from learners and will require the design to integrate interaction and include hands-on activities.

- *Staffing:* When designing an e-learning course, staffing needs are very different from classroom instruction. These needs depend on the context; for example, participants will need and expect different amounts of support (technical or content-related). Some additional considerations include technical staff requirements and availability, and the role of the instructor to guide learners through content and answers.

- *Ethical issues:* This important topic is rarely considered in learning, and it can greatly affect the attitude of learners. Communications should always be at a professional level. Clear communication policies about sexist, racist, or aggressive remarks help ensure that the instruction will not offend any of the participants. Instructors must set rules about confidentiality of discussions, prerequisite knowledge for the course, methods of assessment, and so forth. Learners should agree with the rules before beginning the instruction. Knowing the learners will help determine what rules and policies to set.

- *Group management:* All learners are different, and as such, must be treated differently. Instructors should try to learn key information from learners prior to the start of the instruction. Most instructors will make some adjustments to the group tactics once the instruction begins. By planning ahead, fewer adjustments will have to be made later in managing communications between learners, assigning them to teams, and motivating participation.

WLP professionals must never underestimate the importance of knowing the learners. Crucial information for the design, development, and delivery of instruction can be gathered from its context. If the context is disregarded, the instruction may be just another generic endeavor with a high risk of failure. Personalizing the instruction for learners will help them feel that their needs are taken into consideration, and they will respond accordingly.

## Feedback

Providing feedback in instruction helps learners see for themselves whether their performance works as well as it needs to. According to Allen (2003), intrinsic feedback in learning "allows learners to assess if their performance was good and effective or incorrect and ineffective. It doesn't rely on the usual instructor assessment and didactic comment. It doesn't misdirect learners' efforts toward pleasing the instructor, rather than learning essential skills. It doesn't suggest that learning is about getting a good grade or passing a test." Conversely, extrinsic feedback is usually delivered in the form of a direct verbal comment or electronic feedback that doesn't allow for learners to determine if their performance worked or not.

Table 3-1 lists examples of extrinsic and intrinsic feedback for particular learning behaviors.

With intrinsic feedback, the learner immediately knows that he or she has made an error, for example, when seeing the circuit graphically melt as indicated in Table 3-1. Learners can make adjustments based on this feedback and continue to refine their understanding of how a circuit works. According to Allen, intrinsic feedback lends itself naturally to discovery environments; a process can be simulated and the results of the learner's reactions demonstrated.

## Table 3-1. Examples of Extrinsic and Intrinsic Feedback

| Learning Behavior | Typical Extrinsic Feedback | Intrinsic Feedback |
|---|---|---|
| When learning structured management techniques, a learner provides clear objectives to employees. | "That's correct." | Key business indicators show increased profit margins and reduced employee complaints. The boss compliments the learner on his or her work. |
| When learning electronics, a learner mistakenly connects a 400-volt lead to a 12-volt circuit. | "No, that's not the correct power source. What voltage do you need for the 12-volt circuit?" | In an e-learning environment, the circuit graphically melts down with animation and sound. |

## Table 3-2. Participant Learning Preferences

| Method | Gathering Information | | Processing Information | |
|---|---|---|---|---|
| | Active | Passive | Deductive | Inductive |
| Lecture or presentation | | ✓ | ✓ | |
| Group discussion | ✓ | | ✓ | |
| Readings | ✓ | | ✓ | |
| Simulation or role-play | ✓ | | | ✓ |
| Programmed instruction | ✓ | | ✓ | |
| Games | ✓ | | | ✓ |
| Panels | | ✓ | ✓ | |
| Demonstration | | ✓ | | ✓ |
| Case study | ✓ | | ✓ | |

# Active Training Techniques

Active training is an approach to training that ensures that participants are actively involved in the process. Active learning is based on the cooperative learning approach, in which participants learn from each other in pairs or small groups. Some examples of active training include group discussion, games, and simulation or role play.

Adults have different ways of learning. Some gather information actively, some passively. Some are better at processing information inductively, and some learn better through deductive reasoning. Instructional designers, recognizing these differences, include a variety of techniques to address these learning preferences. Table 3-2 indicates how some training methods apply to the different learning preferences.

In the didactic style of training, the instructor generally stands in front of the learners who are supposed to absorb knowledge. In this case, the instructor controls most of the direction and content through a lecture format, and the learners are expected to acquire and retain knowledge primarily through memorization. Research shows, however, that the active learning and a participatory training style is more effective than the didactic style for adult learners. Therefore, determining the most appropriate training styles and devices to use to maintain learner interest and to present certain types of information is important.

Some active training techniques include

- opening exercises

- engaging lectures and lecturettes

- demonstration

- case study
- guided teaching
- group inquiry
- information search
- role playing
- games
- simulations
- writing tasks
- projects
- practicum
- fishbowl
- brainstorming
- buzz groups
- discussions
- programmed learning
- question-and-answer
- reading
- videos
- focus groups
- nominal group techniques
- interviews
- panel discussion
- skits
- job aids
- on-the-job training
- prework for learners.

## Examples of Active Training Techniques

***Engaging lectures:*** This method consists of standing and delivering information. Properly designed, lectures can impart a substantial amount of information to varied groups of learners, but they require superior presentation skills and limit audience participation—which can limit knowledge absorption. One way to supplement a lecture is to assign readings, which can augment the information the instructor provides during the lecture. For maximum effectiveness, the learning professional can encourage learners to break into small groups and analyze what they have read.

***Group discussion:*** Facilitators guide this informal training method, encouraging the learners to share their knowledge and experiences. Imposing a structure on these discussions and limiting them to small groups are important considerations. Although the training professional and the participants can often benefit from the opportunity to contribute to the learning activity, this teaching method can prove time-consuming. Worse yet, sometimes participants may be unresponsive or disruptive, they may talk too much or not enough, or they may monopolize discussions.

***Simulations and role play:*** In this method, trainers assign the participants a situation to mimic to solve a problem. Although this method is not appropriate for large groups or for participants who feel threatened or self-conscious, when used appropriately, it can tackle tough challenges in a short amount of time.

***Games:*** This method employs competitive activities governed by rules that define players' actions and determine outcomes. Games actively involve and engage participants. Facilitators can also use them as icebreakers.

***Demonstrations:*** In this method, the instructor shows learners how to perform a task through a demonstration, a description, and an explanation. Demonstrations stimulate interest and engage the audience's attention. Designers should plan them carefully and limit their use to small groups.

***Case study:*** This method presents a statement of a problem—a case. The group tries to use the case to find solutions for complex issues. This method allows learners to apply new knowledge and skills they have acquired through other instructional methods.

# E-Learning Techniques

Realizing the potential of e-learning will require designing and deploying e-learning projects in ways that clearly and substantially advance organizational goals. E-learning is not a single, one-size-fits-all solution to every problem that besets training. In fact, treating it as such often causes it to fail to deliver the potential benefits it offers. Realizing those benefits requires an understanding of what e-learning can accomplish for an organization and its individual employees and customers. And it requires a clear view of the vast variety of e-learning solutions possible.

Training managers, even zealous e-learning advocates, are recommending more of a surgical approach to e-learning deployments. Rather than promising to replace all conventional training with e-learning within six months, they now suggest targeting the 25 percent best-suited for e-learning and ramping up an additional five to 10 percent per year. Few talk about conducting all training by e-learning, and many now understand the advantages of blended solutions that mix e-learning and conventional methods.

Managers seeking to apply e-learning must do so thoughtfully and carefully. They must take a realistic view of what e-learning can and cannot do. Managers realize that e-learning projects must be anchored on specific performance objectives that stem directly from sanctioned organizational goals.

The design, development, and delivery of e-learning must proceed with those corporate goals in mind. Projects will be evaluated on whether the original business goals were accomplished, and whether the contribution of e-learning to those goals is clear.

Some important ideas about e-learning need special emphasis, either because they correct widespread misconceptions or because they further the more sophisticated use of e-learning required to fulfill its promise. These key ideas include:

- ***E-learning is not just courses.*** E-learning can be packaged in units other than complete courses and can be embedded in, blended with, and infused into other efforts. E-learning lets trainers deliver mini-courses, micro-courses, and nano-courses as they strive to develop truly reusable training components.

- ***E-learning is not always a noun.*** E-learning is sometimes a verb, that is, a process. Sometimes it is an adverb, that is, a way of doing things. E-learning is not a particular program or a single technology. It is, however, a way of using tools and technology to stimulate learning.

- ***E-learning is a collection of processes and technologies.*** E-learning can be embedded in existing organizational systems and activities, including classroom training, online help, performance support systems, and knowledge management efforts. E-learning is considered a constituent in such efforts rather than just a stand-alone project.

- ***E-learning is a solution in search of a problem.*** E-learning seldom works well when it is the end rather than the means. Organizations must focus on the ends of training before selecting e-learning as the means.

When creating e-learning instruction, several considerations should be incorporated into the design including simulations and authentic tasks, feedback, and navigation best practices.

## Simulations

Computer-based simulators are devices that duplicate the essential features of a task and enable people to practice the task. They provide learners with a realistic and interactive experience. Simulation immerses the participant in a mocked-up environment where he or she can practice tasks to master skills and gain understanding. Simulations can provide participants with hands-on experience. It is not always economical, safe, or possible to have participants perform tasks while they are learning; simulations enable a close approximation.

Like other forms of e-learning, simulations can greatly reduce average learning time, and therefore, the cost associated with learning. In computer-based business simulation applications, for example, a virtual workplace is created, and the participants perform the tasks that they will have to perform on the job, such as starting a company, creating a production strategy, or defending an investment plan to a board of directors. Unexpected events or changes in the business climate arise that the participants must resolve. For example, the participants can attempt to recover from poor cash positions, labor disputes, and manufacturing snafus, without risking the financial health of a real company. Simulation exposes the participants to a broad array of scenarios in a short period of time, and they can see the results of decisions play out in a few seconds, so it's easier to relate to outcomes. One feature of business simulations is the use of simulated personalities that interact with the participants.

Allen notes the importance of using authenticity in simulations to engage learners. "Learning tasks must be authentic—they must relate directly to the effective performance of tasks on the job. Authentic tasks are far more appealing than almost any rhetorical or academic task. They heighten our propensity to get involved." Without the context provided by such authenticity, learners have trouble incorporating what they have learned.

Designing a case analysis or game-based simulation requires the designer to complete the following key tasks (these also apply to classroom simulations):

- ***Clarify learning objectives.*** In other words, the designer must identify what participants should be able to do as a result of completing the simulation and sequence these performance objectives from simple to complex.

- ***Distill key learning content.*** Incorporating key learning content into a skill guide, worksheet with analysis questions, decision flow chart, matrix of relationships, or other performance support tool that presents a conceptual framework is helpful. These tools also can serve as a guide during the simulation as well as a follow-up tool after training.

- ***Identify challenges that will compel learners to practice applying the objectives.*** The designer must also identify the types of people involved in the simulation, including a typical range of personal styles, motivations, and preferences.

- ***Add individuality.*** Each case situation or conversation needs to showcase people who have their own objectives and personalities, which may conflict with learners. For example, a very analytical customer might become irritated with any responses by a sales representative that offer anecdotes rather than statistics. Meanwhile, a customer who values interpersonal relationships may become irritated with sales representatives who recite statistics rather than case examples of other customers.

- ***Build in the elements of a good game.*** These elements include goals, behaviors to achieve goals, obstacles, rewards and consequences (in the form of points), constants, change, and variables.

## E-Learning Feedback

E-learning often includes some form of simulation to provide feedback. In Table 3-1, one example of this type of e-learning feedback was presented: the graphic representation of the circuit melting down. When feedback is included in the instruction, Allen suggests that it may be wise for learners to rate their own performance and to state their plans for improvement.

In e-learning environments where intrinsic feedback cannot be relayed, extrinsic feedback is rarely as helpful as designers would like in conveying useful information. Intrinsic feedback provides the learner with a clear message regarding the correctness of the response as well as more meaningful information about how the response should be adjusted. The e-learning designer should build in mechanisms that enable intrinsic feedback for effective learning.

## Navigation Best Practices

While there are dozens of models and approaches to teaching and learning, there are two major frameworks from which to view training and education. In the first, content and knowledge is determined and distributed to learners via lecture, textbook, videotape, or some other way. In the second framework, the learners transform information, generate hypotheses, and make decisions about the knowledge they are constructing or socially constructing through communication with others (Berge 1998; McManus 1996).

Designers motivate learners through external stimuli, such as a multimedia webpage with graphics, sound, or animation, and an inquiry, such as an interesting problem or mystery to be solved. However, a designer's key focus still needs to be on the relevance of what is to be learned and the perceived needs of the learners.

Some e-learning instruction is designed linearly with learners only being allowed to perform the next step in front of them or to quit the instruction.

As Allen points out, good navigation is just the opposite. It provides learners as many controls as reasonably possible and helps learners feel that they have almost unlimited control—or at least the control they could realistically want. Navigation ties together the structural components at many different levels, much like the trunk of a tree with many limbs—the leaves representing the possible interactions available on each branch.

Allen outlines a list of navigation design imperatives that are often misapplied or frequently overlooked—and which usually make e-learning more effective—when applied correctly. These imperatives include

- ***Letting learners see the boundary of their universe:*** Adults like to know the purpose of activities and to decide whether to complete the activity now or later, and in what order. They like to gain some perspective, consider their options, and decide whether to make a commitment or search for other options. Therefore, when applying this to e-learning, adults are more likely to have a better experience if they have an opportunity to confirm how long the instruction will take, the content to be covered, and the level of difficulty.

- ***Orienting learners to the size and time commitment required:*** Many designers immediately launch into instruction after reviewing the learning objectives; however, learners may not have a sense of the e-learning characteristics (such as how big is it or what type of information is included). With books, learners can quickly see how many pages are included, the type of information provided, the size of the print, how many pictures are included, and the usefulness of the index and glossary. E-learning designers should do everything possible to give a quick, positive impression of the instruction and enable users to quickly jump into the heart of the content as well as to provide time estimates of how long the instruction is likely to take.

- ***Letting learners see how the content is organized:*** Providing learners with an overview of the content organization helps to orient them to where they currently are and provides a wealth of information about the content itself—primarily the sequencing of the content. For example, the concepts may be presented from easy to hard, chronologically, by discipline, or based on dependencies and relationships, and so forth. Designers may have to make tough decisions on presenting content to allow quick and easy access to information without requiring learners to drill down to many hierarchical layers in the instruction.

- ***Letting learners see where they are:*** Once learners are in an e-learning experience, they may lose their bearings quickly. Allen suggests many creative ways to help orient learners to where they are in the instruction, for example, a thermometer or dot that progresses as the instruction is completed.

- ***Letting learners go forward:*** When designing e-learning, designers should not make learners navigate backward through a series of submenus to go forward. While this might be justified by saying it helps learners to understand the structure, providing learners with a reminder of the overall structure without making them navigate backward minimizes learner frustration.

- ***Letting learners back up:*** Learners occasionally may think they have mastered key points, only to find out later that they do not understand a basic concept. Designing e-learning with the ability for learners to back up provides an optimal learning experience and enables adult learners to take responsibility for their own learning.

- ***Letting learners correct themselves:*** Adult learners derive a great deal of satisfaction by privately discovering that they have made a mistake and then fixing it on their own. As Allen notes, "The outcome includes knowing what happens when you do the right thing. Instead of being told what to do, adult learners find the path and appreciate it in all its nuances more than by simply following step-by-step instructions . . . [while this may make some extra work] it takes work to provide intrinsic feedback through which learners see the consequences of their choices directly," rather than being told "No, that's not correct" from the instruction.

---

## Navigation Provides

Abilities to preview and personally assess

- what can be learned and the structure of the content
- how valuable it will be
- how difficult it will be.

Abilities to

- select and list menus and submenus (if any)
- determine if any prerequisites exist and whether they have been met
- go to and back out of selected items
- determine where the learner is within the structure
- access help on using the application.

When accessing instructional help, glossaries, reference material, or other resources, the ability to

- back up, review, skip ahead, preview, and return
- back up and try different answers or questions
- bookmark and return to points of interest or concern
- call up services, such as glossaries or examples
- restart and resume where the instruction was stopped.

Once the learning has begun, abilities to determine

- how much has been accomplished and how much remains to be learned
- the scores or mastery levels earned.

The ability to review many performance details, such as

- how much time was spent in each activity
- how many trials were necessary for the initial success
- how many practice sessions occurred
- what the scores on the practice sessions were.

Source: Allen (2003). Web-Based Learning

---

Tools such as videophone conferencing and computer-based training (CBT) have been around for years. When, then, would an organization need to find new ways or use new technology? The answer is simple: For the global workforce to remain competitive, organizations and learners must work in real time, in multinational arenas, and with multiple formats of information. The medium that supports a company's desire for competitive advantage is the World Wide Web.

With this relatively new medium and continually expanding technology, it is important to understand the process of sound instructional design that, when applied to the web, can facilitate a great learning experience.

To address the preceding business challenge, organizations must have a process in place that

- analyzes customers and business behavior

- adapts technology design and delivery to facilitate learner satisfaction by anticipating a learner's current business and technology environment and future learning needs

- uses a process that enables training developers to create, design, develop, implement, evaluate, and measure customer satisfaction.

When designing instruction for the web, designers use the same ADDIE model and tools as are used for any other instruction. However, designing web-based training (WBT) presents several special considerations and opportunities. There are many questions that organizations, as well as individuals, need to answer before using the web to instruct learners. Some of the additional things to consider when designing instruction for the web include

- authoring systems

- content management systems

- delivery systems

- learner analysis

- media analysis

- web-based project team analysis

- task analysis

- web usability

- graphic design.

## ✓ **Chapter 3 Knowledge Check**

1.  **The instructional design of a virtual live session on handling difficult customers for a call center is primarily based on which of the following inputs?**

    ___ A.  Needs assessment of training requirements and learning objectives

    ___ B.  Call center representatives' frequency and types of interactions

    ___ C.  Learner attitudes and motivation to learn about dealing with customers

    ___ D.  Ethical issues and staffing in the call center

2.  **An in-depth analysis of the characteristics of potential learners for a change management course will most likely *not* include investigation of which of the following?**

    ___ A.  Motivational factors

    ___ B.  Education

    ___ C.  Cultural background

    ___ D.  Media

3.  **Using games as a part of instruction is most beneficial to what type of learner?**

    ___ A.  Adults who gather information passively

    ___ B.  Deductive information processors

    ___ C.  Adults who gather information actively

    ___ D.  Visual information processors

4.  **Which of the following best describes simulations?**

    ___ A.  An exercise that includes a form of real-life situation so participants can practice making decisions and analyze the results of those decisions

    ___ B.  An exercise that shows learners how to perform a task through a demonstration, a description, or an explanation

    ___ C.  An exercise that presents a statement of a problem in which the group tries to use the problem to find solutions to complex issues

    ___ D.  An exercise encouraging learners to share their knowledge and experiences in small-group discussions

**5. Which type of feedback should be designed into an e-learning course in which learners are learning customer service skills?**

   __ A. Extrinsic

   __ B. Intrinsic

   __ C. Delayed

   __ D. Realistic

# References

Allen, M.W. (2003). *Michael Allen's Guide to E-Learning*. Hoboken, NJ: John Wiley & Sons.

Beal, T.T. (May 9, 2003). "Simulations on a Shoestring." *Learning Circuits*. Alexandria, VA: ASTD Press.

Biech, E. (2005). *Training for Dummies®*. Hoboken, NJ: Wiley Publishing.

Carliner, S. (1995). *Every Object Tells a Story: A Grounded Model of Design for Object-Based Learning in Museums*. Doctoral dissertation. Atlanta, GA: Georgia State University.

————— . (2002). *Designing E-Learning*. Alexandria, VA: ASTD Press.

————— . (2003). *Training Design Basics*. Alexandria, VA: ASTD Press.

Gillespie Myers, J. (2005). "How to Select and Use Learning Tools." *Infoline* No. 250507.

Harris, P.M., and O.S. Castillo. (2002). "Instructional Design for WBT." *Infoline* No. 250202.

Hodell, C. (1999). "Lesson Design and Development." *Infoline* No. 258906.

Horton, W. (2002). *Using E-Learning*. Alexandria, VA: ASTD Press.

Kirkpatrick, D.L. (1998). *Evaluating Training Programs: The Four Levels*. 2nd edition. San Francisco: Berrett-Koehler.

Mantyla, K. (2001). *Blending E-Learning*. Alexandria, VA: ASTD Press.

McArdle, G.E. (1999). *Training Design and Delivery*. Alexandria, VA: ASTD Press.

Mohn, C.G., S. Field, and G. Frank. (2000). "Virtual Reality: Is It for You?" In G. Piskurich, P. Beckschi, and B. Hall, eds., *The ASTD Handbook of Training Design and Delivery*. New York: McGraw-Hill.

Price, J., and L. Price. (2002). *Hot Text: Web Writing That Works*. Indianapolis: New Riders.

Russo, C.S., ed. (2003). "Basic Training for Trainers." *Infoline* No. 258808.

Sheinberg, M. (October, 2001). "Know Thy Learner: The Importance of Context in E-Learning Design." *Learning Circuits*. Alexandria, VA: ASTD Press.

# 4
# Delivery Options and Media

 Regardless of the setting, adult educators must recognize the many different avenues of delivery. Each avenue has inherent characteristics that all trainers should be comfortable with. Each avenue has different learner demographics and different motivations. It is valuable for the facilitator to understand the different delivery options so that he or she can have some control over the delivery of the content and also provide insight into the content by making recommendations as to its delivery.

To better understand the distinction between presentation methods and distribution methods, think of the various ways someone could get a message to a friend in a distant country. The ***presentation method*** may take a number of different formats, including text, pictures, symbols, and sounds.

For each presentation method, one or more distribution methods exists for actually transmitting the formatted message to the friend. These ***distribution methods*** include email, telegram, fax, phone call, and videotape.

Certain presentation methods may only be transmitted using one distribution method (for example, a telegram distributed via telegraph), whereas others can have an array of distribution options (such as a letter distributed using fax, air mail, or express mail). Some restrictions may prevent a person from using a certain type of distribution method. For instance, overnight courier services may not service the friend's country.

Regardless of the process chosen, the decision ultimately pairs a presentation method with a distribution method.

## Learning Objective:

☑ Discuss the factors that need to be considered in the appropriate selection of presentation methods and media for learning.

## Key Knowledge: Selecting Delivery Options and Media

Although some people express concern that e-learning might spell the end of classroom training or that it is inferior to classroom training, e-learning ultimately will complement it. Workplace Learning and Performance (WLP) professionals use classroom training for what it does best and do likewise for e-learning.

*E-learning* is outstanding for teaching rote skills; it has the infinite patience needed to do so. With the privacy of the computer, slower learners can have the extensive remediation they need, and fast learners can speed through a course, unencumbered by their classmates. E-learning is also an excellent tool for teaching prerequisite material. Instructors can require learners to take a prerequisite course and pass a pretest before coming to the classroom. In that way, the instructor can begin the classroom course at a higher level, sure that each learner has completed the prerequisite learning. As a result, the classroom course can provide an in-depth learning experience, a shorter learning experience, or both.

E-learning should not be used when the technology analysis indicates that the current equipment and infrastructure are not adequate to support the bandwidth and other technology needs required by the various types of e-learning. Nor should it be used if participants' self-directedness is low or if they are "technologically challenged" and may have issues accessing the content.

*Classroom learning* provides an opportunity to develop higher-order thinking skills and stimulate interpersonal exchanges. Although these goals can be accomplished online through simulations and asynchronous learning, they often have more effect with learners in the classroom.

In some cases, classroom training might not be the most efficient way to address knowledge and skill deficiencies. These are the drawbacks of classroom training:

• Training is expensive.

• Training is hard to schedule.

• Training is temporary. Learners don't retain knowledge or skills unless they have an opportunity to practice.

If possible, a trainer should consider a blended approach to help provide learners with all the skills and knowledge needed to perform effectively on the job. *Blended learning* describes the practice of using several media in one curriculum. It typically refers to the combination of classroom instruction and any type of training that includes self-directed use of online capabilities. Some additional solutions include job aids, performance support systems, and self-directed learning programs.

For more information, see Module 2, *Delivering Training*, Chapter 4, "Training Delivery Options and Media."

# 5
# Job and Task Analysis

 Careful exploration of needs is a critical aspect of designing effective training. Learning and development professionals should know a wide range of approaches to job and task analysis and be able to choose the most appropriate analysis for each project. Outcomes of this analysis drive key deliverables of the needs assessment phase, including objectives, activities, and delivery method.

*Job analysis* is the process used to break a job into its component duty or functional areas and the task statements associated with those duty areas. The key deliverable of the job analysis is a validated task list. This task list is a critical deliverable because it can be used as the foundation to create multiple derivative products, including curriculum design, behavioral interview guides, self-assessment tools, organizational assessments, job descriptions, and competency models.

A variety of techniques, methods, and tools are available to conduct a job analysis. In many cases, the human resources' compensation unit has developed standard procedures for these analyses. Knowledge of the job-analysis process and the various methods and tools used can facilitate the career-planning and talent-management processes by identifying the knowledge, skills, abilities, work behaviors, and education required for various jobs within a career path. This knowledge can help an organization identify and improve its talent force.

The key for the WLP professional is to understand the job-analysis process. That way he or she can help people identify the skills, knowledge, abilities, work behaviors, and education that are crucial for developing their careers and preparing for specific jobs within that career. Generally, a human resource compensation specialist handles the major responsibility for this area. But, it is important for the WLP professional to work closely with the compensation expert and understand which method is most appropriate for the various jobs.

## Learning Objective:

☑ Describe the difference between a job and task analysis and the role of each in designing instruction.

# Key Knowledge: Job and Task Analysis

*Job analysis* is an important tool in the WLP professionals' toolbox. Job analysis is crucial in helping individuals develop their careers and in helping organizations develop employees and maximize their talent.

A job analysis is more detailed than a job description and less detailed than a task analysis. Job descriptions generally explain the duties of a job but do not list the specific tasks that a job performer must do to fulfill the stated duties. A *task analysis*, however, examines a single task within a job and breaks it down into the actual steps of performance. Task analysis is about the *how* of a job, whereas job analysis is focused on the *what*.

Job analysis identifies all duties and the respective tasks done on a daily, weekly, monthly, and yearly basis that make up a single job function. A thorough job analysis results in a complete picture of the job, including duties, tasks (ranked by select factors), general knowledge, and skills required to be successful, and resources needed to perform the job effectively.

A complete job analysis can take the form of a map—and it functions exactly like that—a map to approach whatever goal the employee must achieve. Job analysis identifies the duties and tasks that make up a single job function. Think of a job as the 20,000-foot view, tasks are at 5,000 feet, and individual steps taken within each task are at sea level.

Task analysis seeks to identify the knowledge and skills necessary to do a job. A task has a beginning and an end; consists of two or more steps; results in a specific, measurable output (either a decision, product, or service); and can be performed independently of other tasks.

A job can have many tasks. The amount of task information to capture in a job analysis depends on the business needs. One might elect to capture tasks down to the administration level (such as, make copies) or choose to focus on meatier tasks (such as, analyze and interpret the weekly sales numbers) that represent the bulk of the job in question.

The advantage of a task analysis is it makes note of the minute details of the specific tasks required of a job. One disadvantage is that it can be time-consuming to collect this detailed data.

A job analysis helps practitioners identify the required competencies and categorize jobs according to such requirements. Three competency elements that constitute most positions include managerial or administrative, supervisory, and functional skills or knowledge.

For more information, see Module 9, *Career Planning and Talent Management*, Chapter 3, "Job Analysis Tools and Procedures."

# 6
# Content Knowledge From SMEs

At the core of every learning program is its content, and designers must already know the core content, or they must be adept at eliciting appropriate content from subject matter experts (SMEs) or thoroughly researching topics from a range of sources. When a project requires unique content, the following guidelines will help the learning professional work with SMEs to identify and gather appropriate content. Information on researching topics is covered in more detail in Chapter 7, "Assessment Methods and Formats," and in Module 4, *Measuring and Evaluating*.

## Learning Objective:

☑ Describe several techniques for using SMEs to help convey key information used during the instructional design process.

Chapter 6

# Collaboration With SMEs to Identify Instructional Needs

As Goldsmith (2000) points out, the SME is a training project's primary content resource. The best SMEs have deep knowledge or experience relative to the target deliverable and can communicate that knowledge effectively. They also are able to quickly understand the learning program's objectives and how to reach them. The value of an SME depends on his or her understanding of the topic and the number of other available SMEs in the field. From a design team's perspective, the best situation occurs when there are many experts who are all available. More typical is a situation with few experts and almost none are available. When this happens, the SME becomes *the* critical-path resource on the project.

Some instructional designers work with SMEs regularly, whereas others never work with them. Designers fall into three different kinds of roles in curriculum development:

- The designer is the only person involved and is the SME.
- The designer has some content knowledge but works with an SME.
- The designer has little if any content knowledge and relies on the SME for assistance.

The need for SMEs varies with the kind of instructional design. Working with SMEs is an art in itself. The designer's tool of working effectively with SMEs is a valuable one to enhance or develop.

No matter which of these roles applies, designers should use questioning techniques, analysis techniques, data-collection techniques, and interviews to uncover content and to distinguish what needs to be included in the instruction.

## Categories of SMEs

SMEs fall into one of two general categories. Some have expertise in a specific skill, such as painting or electrical work, and are brought on to a project to provide data for apprenticeship materials, procedural manuals, or other aspects of the project. Many of these SMEs have never done any type of design work before. Designers must be sure that they are clear as to what information they are asking the SMEs to provide, especially SMEs who are new to the design process. Working with objectives and evaluations might be new to them, and they must realize that they need only provide technical information and that the designer will take care of the rest.

The other kind of SME is more academic, and the project typically is the result of research or experience gained in the field, or both. Designers bring these SMEs to a project to offer expertise in specialized areas. This group is likely to include professionals with advanced degrees and high academic standing. Clear lines of demarcation and responsibility are vital. The designers in this environment must also have decision-making authority and responsibility for the instructional design process.

96

## Working Relationships

Goldsmith notes that the SME's job is to work with the team to supply or build the content. In some cases, SMEs do this directly by writing the materials themselves. In other cases, they work with the team to develop the content through interviews. Sometimes the content is based on an article, book, or other source the SME has already developed. (For more information on developing content by doing research, see Chapter 7, "Assessment Methods and Formats.") In this case, the SME will work with the team to modify the existing materials.

The team's working relationship with SMEs depends on several factors, including whether the SMEs are

- internal or external

- full-time or part-time

- on site or off site

- business people or academics.

According to Goldsmith,

> As important as all these factors are, the most important factor concerning SMEs is motivation. Motivation is a key issue with all team members, but is especially important with SMEs because, from their point of view, the assignment and/or reporting relationship given to them may not be desirable. For some, participation on a multimedia or Web project may be a sideline, something they do between "real" projects. The assignment is not in their job description or development plan, and they are concerned that they will not be rewarded for their efforts. For others, participation in the project may be viewed as a distraction, something to be finished as quickly as possible so that "real" work can continue. In short, their perception could be that the assignment is trivial, transitory, and unrewarding. To avoid this situation, the team has several options:

- Compensate generously.

- Give the SME increased exposure for his or her work.

- Link the project to the SME's professional advancement.

- Establish a formal relationship.

Goldsmith continues,

> Money is a great motivator, but some SMEs may be just as motivated by an opportunity to increase the audience for their work. In another scenario, the team (specifically management) could tie the success of the project to the SME's professional or career advancement. If the resource is internal, project participation could be added to the job description, with substantial benefits offered at the project's conclusion. If the SME is an external

resource, work on the course could become a significant resume item. Another option is to make SMEs formal partners in a project, perhaps offering them a percentage of the profits or giving them an important reporting relation on the team. Some creative thinking may be necessary to change an SME's negative attitude if these strategies do not work.

With luck, the team may be able to find an SME who is already motivated. If the team is in the more typical situation of few experts with little availability, it needs to find out what the SMEs want and provide it.

For designers to be effective when working with SMEs, they need to understand the learning content as quickly as possible. One way to accomplish this goal is for the designer to prepare all of the materials, interview the SME and seek clarification to questions, and then prepare the instructional materials.

SMEs may not be aware of adult learning theories and instructional design techniques. For this reason, the designer needs to take responsibility for ensuring instructional integrity of the materials. When SMEs are effective communicators, they often mistake communication skills for instructional design skills.

One of the most important keys to working with SMEs is clarity. Most people are eager to work on instructional design projects and just need to know the rules. Everyone likes to have his or her knowledge or experience recognized and used. Working with designers should be a great experience for them, and once they realize that the designers are there to provide the instructional framework, they can relax and concentrate on the content.

## Choice of SMEs

Choosing the right SMEs is critically important. The following rules are a useful guide for designers to make the selection:

- Only use SMEs with recent (one year or less) experience in the content area. The pace of change in most fields is such that people with recent experience are considered current in the field. Every field of study is different, but most change considerably in a year.

- Ask around and find out which SMEs are considered the best by their peers.

- Interview SMEs to reduce the chance of possible personality conflicts.

- Determine if the SMEs have enough time to devote to the design process.

- Determine how SMEs will be compensated before starting.

- Review and resolve any copyright issues with SMEs before starting.

- If relevant, ask for writing samples or previous content-related materials.

- Determine if any previous instructional design experience exists.

Spending a little time to find the best SMEs early in the process may eliminate an irrevocable error later during in the project.

## Roles of SMEs

In summary, Goldsmith points out that the power of excellent training comes not from the subject matter content, but from the ISD process that designs, implements, and evaluates that training. The SME's role within that context is to

- provide expert testimony that can be translated into content

- check the accuracy of all content developed for the application

- work with the designer to ensure that the design and content are compatible.

## ✓ **Chapter 6 Knowledge Check**

1. **Which of the following is *not* one of the basic roles of a designer on a project?**

    __ A.  The designer has little if any content knowledge and relies on the SME to select the most appropriate instructional strategy and media.

    __ B.  The designer is the only person involved and is the SME.

    __ C.  The designer has some subject matter knowledge but works with an SME.

    __ D.  The designer has little if any subject matter knowledge and relies on the SME for assistance.

2. **The primary role of an SME on a project includes all of the following *except***

    __ A.  Works with the team to supply or build the content

    __ B.  Checks the accuracy of the content developed

    __ C.  Establishes the goals of the instruction and supplies the content

    __ D.  Works with the designer to ensure that the design and content are compatible

3. **Which of the following is *not* one of the techniques used by designers when working with SMEs to uncover and to distinguish what needs to be included in the instruction?**

    __ A.  Questioning techniques

    __ B.  Analysis techniques

    __ C.  Evaluation techniques

    __ D.  Data collection techniques and interviews

# References

Elengold, L.J. (2001). "Teach SMEs to Design Training." *Infoline* No. 250106.

Hodell, C. (2000). *ISD From the Ground Up*. Alexandria, VA: ASTD Press.

Goldsmith, J.J. (2000). "Development Teams for Creating Technology-Based Training." In G. Piskurich, P. Beckschi, and B. Hall, eds., *The ASTD Handbook of Training Design and Delivery*. New York: McGraw-Hill.

Russo, C.S. (1999). "Teaching SMEs to Train." *Infoline* No. 259911.

# 7
# Assessment Methods and Formats

Data gathering is a widely used skill in the designer's tool kit. Whether the designer uses it for front-end assessment of needs and context, or back-end evaluation of the effect of training, a designer's skill set must include the ability to design and implement a variety of assessment tools. For data-gathering tools to be effective, a designer must understand key principles related to the use of a range of techniques and how to collate, synthesize, and interpret the resultant information in an open-minded and appropriate way.

Training needs assessment is the process of identifying how training can help an organization reach its goals. Although needs assessment does help training professionals provide input for the ultimate training design, even more important in needs assessment is establishing the presence of a business need, driving a performance need, driving a true training need, identifying the specifics regarding the desired training, and finally, identifying the nontraining issues also present and affecting the performance situation.

## Learning Objectives:

☑ Define needs assessment and discuss the purpose of needs assessment in designing instruction.

☑ List the steps in conducting a training needs assessment.

☑ Describe the differences between an organizational assessment, task assessment, and individual assessment.

☑ Describe the advantages and disadvantages of three data-collection methods.

☑ List five possible results of a needs assessment that the WLP professional might identify.

# The Purpose of Needs Assessment

The classical approach to determining needs or problems is identifying the discrepancy between the desired and actual knowledge, skills, and performance. That discrepancy can translate into the training need. A variety of methods, including interviews, observations, questionnaires, and tests, may lead to identifying needs. Using these methods effectively involves accurately gathering, analyzing, verifying, and reporting data.

Note that needs assessments can be used in a variety of contexts. For example, the goal of a needs assessment in HPI is to discover needs related to performance issues, which can cover a broad variety of topics, such as processes, resources, organizational structures, and so forth. For the purposes of this module, *Designing Learning*, the type of needs assessment under discussion is a training needs assessment. The training needs assessment, when implemented effectively, serves multiple purposes:

- It places the training need or request in the context of the organization's needs. Training adds value only when it ultimately serves a business need.

- It validates and augments the initial issues presented by the sponsor of the training or client. Although sponsors and clients know the business, sometimes they don't know the cause of or the remedy for issues that involve human performance. The needs assessment can reveal different information, provide broader context for the information supplied by the client, and offer different perspectives on the client's initial impressions.

- It ensures that the ultimate training design supports employee performance and thereby helps the organization meet its needs. A significant portion of training needs assessment encompasses gathering information to support the training design, identify and capture current levels of skills and knowledge, and ensure that the design replicates the learners' jobs as closely as possible.

- It results in recommendations regarding nontraining issues that affect achievement of the desired organization and employee performance goals. The main question is this: If the ultimate training program is perfect, what else is going on in the organization that could cause business needs not being met? The needs assessor must identify these issues and provide recommendations to rectify them for several reasons. First, the likelihood of achieving desired business and performance results is much greater. Second, the training function is held accountable only for the business and performance needs that it can affect. Third, identifying additional performance issues increases the value added by the training function to the organization.

- It helps ensure the survival of the training function. When a training program adds value, the training function is valued for its impact and results and is not at high risk during hard times.

- It establishes the foundation for back-end evaluation. Figure 7-1 illustrates how training needs assessment sets the stage for evaluation.

# Figure 7-1. Needs Assessment Relationship to Evaluation

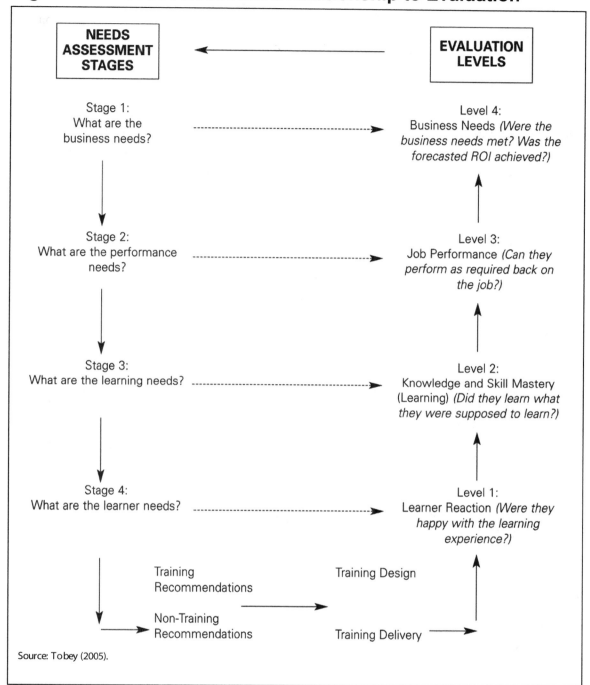

Source: Tobey (2005).

During training needs assessment, measures are taken in four areas (left side of Figure 7-1): business needs, performance needs, learning needs, and learner needs. During evaluation (after training), measurements are taken of the same items, now called the **_four levels of evaluation_**: learner reaction, learning (knowledge and skill mastery), behavior, and results. The goal in training is to identify positive changes in each of the four needs assessment premeasures when they are postmeasured during evaluation.

# Steps to Conduct a Needs Assessment

As with any analysis, there are procedures to be followed to produce a useful product. Here are six steps to help focus the training needs assessment:

## Step 1. Define the Objectives

In this step, the WLP professional determines the purpose and objectives for the training needs assessment. These factors are the bases for management planning and development decisions. Some objectives for conducting training needs assessment include to

- distinguish employees who need training

- identify performance problems, deficiencies, and root causes

- determine whether training is the best solution to problems

- secure the support and commitment of management in the process of building and evaluating effective training programs

- generate data that will be useful in measuring the effect of the training program

- provide specific recommendations for training programs: scope, methods, frequency, cost, and location

- decide priorities for the upcoming year and for long-range strategic planning

- justify spending to top management by determining the value and cost of training—including calculating the difference between no training costs (the expenses incurred or monies lost by continuing with the same problems) and the costs of the training solution.

## Step 2. Identify the Necessary Data

A thorough needs assessment requires information to identify the

- need

- solution

- population requiring training

- strategies for delivering training.

Knowing the nature and quantity of the information required is important for a useful assessment study. WLP professionals may need opinions, attitude surveys, financial statements, job descriptions, performance appraisals, work samples, or historical documents from company archives.

## Step 3. Select Data-Collection Method

In this step, the WLP professional chooses or designs a method for gathering data. He or she uses various combinations of the following methods—alternating between structured and unstructured versions—questionnaires, observations, group discussions, key consultations, work samples, records, reports, and tests.

The practitioner should base structured or formal assessment methods on the necessary data as outlined in Step 2 and also on a comparison of each method's degree of effectiveness for gathering the data. He or she should then validate all instruments (questionnaires, surveys, and so forth) used in this approach.

## Step 4. Collect the Data

If gathering information from sample or study groups, the WLP professional should administer the questionnaires, conduct the interviews, observe performances, and so forth.

## Step 5. Analyze and Confirm the Data

To uncover problems and related trends or patterns, the practitioner should compare the new data with past years' information. He or she then confirms results and checks for accuracy by consulting with the persons who originally provided the information.

## Step 6. Prepare the Final Report

In this step, the WLP professional points out problems, needs, weak areas, and recommended strategies for improvement. Using tables, graphs, and other support data for findings, he or she designs a clear and interesting presentation with well-written materials and attractive visuals.

### Nailing Down Needs Assessments

Although disagreements exist among WLP professionals about needs assessments, most experts recognize the following:

- It comes at the beginning of any systematic approach to training, prior to teaching anybody anything in any setting or using any technology.

- The learning professional carries out a needs assessment to understand more about a performance problem—some gap between what is happening and what ought to be happening. This means that needs assessment is the systematic search for details about the difference between optimal and actual.

- A lot of verbal support exists for the idea of needs assessment, far more than for the time and resources it takes to do well. When people want learning professionals to solve problems, they want them solved yesterday. If a needs assessment stands between the problem and a snappy new course, needs assessment tends to be viewed as suspect.

## Nailing Down Needs Assessments, continued

- People who conduct needs assessments usually do so by using in-person and telephone interviews and questionnaires. Most training literature agrees on the leading characteristics of these two techniques: ease of data analysis, anonymity, opportunity to follow up, responses, and cost.

- A needs assessment usually asks for people's feelings. The inquiry should focus on what sources feel is causing the performance problem and whether the learners could perform successfully under pressure. Training resources should not be used on problems that better supervision or powerful incentive plans can dispatch.

- Training, and therefore needs assessment, is not about performance problems as much as it used to be. Now it is about new systems and technologies, necessitating expanded ways of understanding the situation before training.

## General Needs Analysis Guidelines

Following are a number of guidelines for WLP professionals to keep in mind as they undertake a needs analysis. Although all of these suggestions may not be appropriate for every situation, many can help ease the task and simplify the process:

- Use a comprehensive and flexible approach. A good needs analysis should address the total organization, a department, a division, a group, or a single individual.

- Plan a well-timed analysis. Learning professionals should not schedule assessments during difficult periods of structural change, transfer of ownership or executive management, or major policy revisions that affect all organizational levels. Analysts must assess the current needs of individual departments and divisions on their own terms but also on the basis of how these groups can be affected by change in other areas of the organization.

- Use analysis to indicate whether an actual, significant problem or need exists and, if it does, to develop an appropriate solution. The first step is to identify the concerned members of the organization:

  - Why are they interested in the problem?

  - How do they perceive the problem?

  - Why do they support training as a solution?

To determine which individuals are responsible for that problem or need, learning professionals begin at the top of the organizational structure and continue through the lower levels. They include the concerned individuals in every step of the process who must assist in determining the needs and approve the analysis results.

- Know the study subjects. To reduce the possibility of prescribing inappropriate training, the practitioner analyzes the performance level of the target group by identifying discrepancy factors, which are the important differences between high and lower performers. This information is used to determine training program content and emphasis. The WLP professional should enhance strong points discovered during the analysis.

- Vary techniques for gathering data. Habitual use of a few approaches may trap the learning professional in inappropriate applications. Several kinds of independent performance studies are more likely to produce accurate needs assessments than one. For example, surveys may indicate a number of needs, but multiple group or one-on-one interviews may negate those findings.

- Keep studies short. Surveying a small sample of high and low performers is preferable to attempting an analysis of the entire workforce. Large-scale studies create unrealistic expectations of the WLP professional's work and high costs for the sponsor. One good rule is that studies should be completed within 20 to 40 working days.

- View front-end analysis costs as an investment in the future. Strong technical skills; effective assessment methods; accurate scoring; and a lucid, substantial final report are vital for successful analyses. Training professionals should always schedule enough time to prepare a good presentation of their needs analysis results, even if they must stop the process before completing some additional data analyses. At the end, spending time and money on clarifying is better than hastily constructing a presentation.

- In reports and presentations, convey the right amount of information to the appropriate audience at the appropriate time. Reports are typically long and comprehensive, indicating results of surveys, questionnaires, and other methods for gathering data. They may also include explanations of methods and samples of data-gathering devices. Adding an executive summary at the beginning of a lengthy report may be helpful to orient the audience to important points.

## Needs Analysis Planning Checklist

Unfortunately, many companies lose time, effort, and funds on unsuccessful needs studies, and all too often, their failures can be traced to poor planning. Sound decisions at the beginning guarantee a strong foundation throughout the analysis. WLP professionals can make wise choices by thinking through the following issues:

- Who is being trained? What are their job functions? Are they from the same department or from a variety of areas in the organization?

- What are their deficiencies? Why are they deficient?

**Needs Analysis Planning Checklist, continued**

- What are the objectives of the needs analysis? How will a needs analysis assist in solving problems and benefit the organization?

- What are the expected outcomes? Will these outcomes have a persuasive effect on many organizational levels (departmental, divisional, regional, and corporate)?

- Will questionnaires, surveys, tests, interviews, and so forth, or a combination be most appropriate? Who will administer these—in-house personnel or external consultants?

- Will the analysis interrupt the work process? What effect will this have on the workforce and on productivity?

- Will there be a confidentiality policy for handling information?

# Levels of Needs Assessment

The three levels of needs assessment are organizational assessment, task assessment, and individual assessment. Each level is discussed in the sections that follow.

## Organizational Assessment

As the learning professional prepares his or her analysis, he or she must analyze the learning needs and interests of the organization. What are the organization's needs and interests, present and future? What are the learners' needs in the organizational context?

Proactive companies often use a future-oriented assessment. When the company is changing course, launching a new line, or considering succession planning, an organizational assessment is recommended. As part of this organizational assessment, the WLP professional should be sure to detail any knowledge, skills, or abilities that employees will need to know in the future, as their jobs and the organization change.

Both formal and informal assessments of organizational needs are useful. To informally assess organizational needs, the learning professional can take a few minutes to review the latest revision of the organization's mission and goals, along with any unit or departmental goal statements or priorities. Alertness at meetings and in conversations with organizational leaders and careful observation of problem areas or potential areas of growth within the organization also constitute valuable inputs for the organizational needs assessment.

Another component to leverage for the organizational assessment is organizational projections. If, for example, new computer equipment or programs will be put to use within a few months, a means of preparing for this change may need to be incorporated as well.

# Task Assessment

At one time, working for an organization was a marvelously predictable thing. People entered the workforce after they completed whatever level of schooling their aptitudes, inclinations, and finances dictated. They began at the bottom rung of the mythical career ladder and worked their way up.

Jobs in those days were well defined and documented in formal job descriptions that delineated the KSAs required for success in each position. With jobs and job progression so well defined, the instructional designer's task was equally well structured.

Task assessment (or task analysis) is defined as the systematic identification of several items that are necessary to perform any job:

- specific skills
- knowledge
- tools
- conditions
- requirements.

In the past, instructional designers relied on formal job descriptions as the basis for beginning a task analysis. The job descriptions, which often were written after the completion of a job analysis, defined the specific tasks and duties of the position. The designer's job, in essence, was to translate the requirements of the job, as noted in the job analysis and job description documents, into training materials and then to train employees to successfully perform the job.

This process has no flaws in its logic. Indeed, many organizations still follow it as a way to develop support materials and programs needed to ensure optimal job performance. But more and more, the business mantras of improved speed, performance, and process all but do away with the formal definitions of jobs and the rigidity of organizational job tables and progression steps.

A designer must do the following for a task assessment to be complete and detailed enough to develop an appropriate learning:

- Identify the employee proficiency issue or the new skills employees need to learn to conduct their job.
- Examine the job in detail to identify its component tasks.
- Compare job requirements with employee knowledge and skills to identify areas in need of improvement and review job descriptions and specifications for the expected performance and required skills.
- Identify tasks that must be performed and the conditions under which they must be performed.
- Document when and how the tasks are performed.

- Note the quality and quantity of performance required.

- Analyze where and how these skills and knowledge are best acquired.

Task analysis can vary in complexity and scope. For instance, a learning professional could accurately document a simple set of tasks by interviewing current employees, if they were performing the tasks successfully to performance standards. However, the learning professional may require many interviews and data-gathering sessions to identify all the components of a complex job or a position that was undergoing change and did not currently exist in a well-understood manner. Regardless of the level of complexity, task analyses share several fundamental steps:

1. Identifying the major or critical outputs of the job will help the task analyst identify the major tasks and task groupings.

2. Breaking down the major tasks into subtasks or steps is complete when an employee would be able to achieve the goal or result of the task by completing all the steps or subtasks.

3. Determining the type of tasks and subtasks involves distinguishing between

   - ***knowledge tasks,*** also known as cognitive tasks, which require the participant to acquire knowledge, information, or understanding

   - ***skills tasks,*** also known as action tasks or behavior tasks, which require a change in behavior or an action on the part of the participant.

4. Collecting all the data necessary is required to document the tasks and subtasks. Using a variety of data sources increases the validity of the data. The learning professional should ensure each task has a discernible output or result.

5. Validating the data by confirming information derived from interviews through direct observation. Similarly, the learning professional can validate observation logs by reviewing them with SMEs. Direct observation or employee reviews can verify formal job descriptions or job analyses.

6. Obtaining review and approval of task analysis from sponsors, training management, or other management in the organization is important. The task analyst should provide management with the opportunity to modify the scope of the tasks, if needed.

7. Finalizing the reporting of the task analysis is the next step. The format depends on the use of the data. For the final result, the analyst can generate tables, flow-charts, and narrative descriptions, in the detail needed.

8. Distributing findings to management for final approval is the final step. Once approved, the task assessment is complete.

## Individual Assessment

A task assessment focuses on a job and its tasks and identifies the knowledge and skills required to perform the job appropriately. An individual assessment focuses specifically on how a person conducts his or her job. Individual assessments are often used for employee appraisals but also can be used—quite successfully—in training design.

During this process, the instructional designer reviews how a specific person conducts his or her job. In particular, the designer focuses on individual employees and how they do their jobs successfully by pinpointing key activities that a successful employee uses to get his or her job done correctly. At times, performance review data may also be used during this type of assessment. The end result of an individual analysis is to create a development plan designed to help the employee improve performance.

# Data-Collection Methods

Data-collection methods include tools such as questionnaires, tests, checklists, surveys, and scales that systematically gather data about individual groups or entire organizations. In a needs analysis, they indicate both weak and strong areas. To determine their data requirements, WLP professionals consider some of the following questions:

- What are the stated goals or expectations of the employees being studied? How do they relate to organizational goals?

- What is the organizational climate?

- What are the backgrounds and educational profiles of the personnel being studied?

- Who will administer, score, and interpret the results?

- Does the use of follow-up instruments require special training? If so, is this training available?

- Is the scoring objective, or will it require special skills? (Objective scoring eliminates the need for such skills, and respondents more easily accept the results as accurate.)

- How complicated is the scoring? (Complex scoring scales are costly and time-consuming.)

These questions can help the learning professional determine his or her data-collection needs, enabling him or her to select the method(s) that best suit the needs, time constraints, and budget requirements. Data-collection methods need to be analyzed for their strengths and weaknesses so that potential methods for each data source can be identified. Data-collection methods include assessments and tests, performance audits, competency modeling, observation, interviews, focus groups, surveys, work samples, and extant data. Following a discussion of these is a discussion of statistical considerations.

## Quantitative and Qualitative Data

Data-collection methods are either quantitative or qualitative. Quantitative methods are those that result in what is called **hard data**. Hard data is objective and measurable, whether stated in terms of frequency, percentage, proportion, or time. Qualitative measures yield **soft data**. These types of measures are more intangible, anecdotal, personal, and subjective. Examples include opinions, attitudes, assumptions, feelings, values, and desires. Qualitative data cannot be objectified, and that is the characteristic that makes this type of data valuable. For example, knowing how job performers feel (qualitative measure) about a skill will be just as important in the ultimate training design as knowing how well (quantitative measure) they perform it.

Quantitative and qualitative measures can be combined in a data-collection process with excellent results. For example, learning professionals can use a qualitative method (interviews, for example) to collect anecdotes and examples. Then they can develop a quantitative method (a survey, for example), using the collected anecdotes and examples as survey items, and measure how many respondents fit the examples and how frequently the examples fit the respondents. Conversely, a quantitative method can be used first to collect information on frequency and number of respondents. Then a qualitative method can be used to flesh out the survey items with richer detail. Qualitative and quantitative measures can also be combined in the same measurement tool. For example, items on a survey can be qualitative terms, such as feelings and opinions. How many times each is chosen (frequency) is a quantitative measure.

## Assessments and Tests

Assessments and tests gauge what the respondents know, can do, or believe in relation to the training need being investigated. Types of assessments include

- knowledge assessments through verbal or written responses to multiple-choice, true-or-false, fill-in-the-blank, or essay questions
- actual performance of a job skill while being observed
- analysis of work results, product, or output against quality criteria.

Assessments and tests are most often used to gauge current learner knowledge, skill, or performance levels. Table 7-1 presents some advantages and disadvantages of assessments and tests.

When constructing a test, formulating questions and measurement criteria carefully to ensure they are clear is critical. Learning professionals may want to consider using an expert in test writing to ensure validity beyond pilot testing if the content is highly technical, or if they will be limited in using other methods to corroborate the needs assessment outcome. The learning professional should pilot the assessment with a small sample of the population to make sure it is valid and reliable. The learning professional

## Table 7-1. Advantages and Disadvantages of Assessments and Tests

| Advantages | Disadvantages |
|---|---|
| • They are objective.<br><br>• They specifically identify the gap between current and desired performance, knowledge, and skills.<br><br>• The ultimate training design focuses on a specific gap rather than on generalized information. | • Assessments don't always get to the thought processes behind why a participant performed in a certain way.<br><br>• Some participants can "freeze" and perform poorly due to test anxiety.<br><br>• It can be challenging to include both knowledge and skill tests or assessments due to time constraints in the training. |

may also want to consider accompanying a test or assessment with an interview to yield more complete data.

## Performance Audit

Learning professionals use performance audits when performance criteria are clear and sufficient data is available to measure the performance criteria. This method seeks to identify the efficiency and effectiveness of employees. Performance appraisals may also be used to review how well employees have performed in the past. The advantage of this approach is that the training topics and goals are easier to determine. The designer looks at the gap between the criteria and actual performance. The disadvantage of this approach is that the data may be confounded by other variables, such as equipment downtime or external expectations.

## Competency Modeling

A major trend in ISD is the competency-based, functional-content approach, as described in the writings of Tom Sticht, Larry Mickulecky, and others (Sharpe 1997). This approach focuses on the learner, with heavy emphasis on individual learning plans.

These are features of the competency-based approach:

- Occupational analysis identifies competencies (performance objectives) required for successful performance.

- The validity of competencies is verified through people who actually perform the job.

- Criteria (standards) for adequate or excellent performance and the conditions under which the job is to be performed are made known to learners from the beginning.

- The learner and trainer plan individual instruction and evaluation for each competency.

Although certain KSAs may be evaluated, the main measure of success is performance that integrates KSAs under job conditions.

For a long time, many training professionals acknowledged the appeal of the competency-based approach. However, they resisted it and believed they did not have the resources to use it. Individualized content and pacing were the key sticking points. But from the mid-1970s to the present, resistance has faded as business competition has become global, pressure to prove training's value has increased, and many organizations have faced labor shortages. More important, trainers have discovered that this approach works and can be mandated incrementally in several ways:

- Occupational analysis can be initiated for particular organizational levels, divisions, or departments—or for selected jobs.

- Portions of existing and new courses can be individualized.

- Some new courses can be fully competency-based.

Training professionals also have found that occupational analyses are quicker and easier when they fine-tune the initial analytical process to organizational culture and build an updatable information base. The competency-based approach originally applied to relatively separate and sequential tasks. Now, however, learning researchers are studying how the competency-based approach applies to complex learning, such as learning related to leadership and interpersonal relations.

Many experts believe that the competency-based approach should replace the traditional approach to design and development. They disparage the conventional process of gathering and analyzing content information, listing topics, developing and sequencing course objectives, preparing a course description, and developing unit and lesson plans.

Many, however, see that it is not an either/or situation and understand the value of adapting competency-based principles to the traditional process. Most important, however, is the recognition that learning—not just instruction—must be planned.

## Functional-Context Learning

The term *functional context* often crops up in discussions of the competency-based approach. It too describes training that relates to actual job circumstances because training is successful only when learners can carry out learned tasks at their actual workstations. For example, a learner may be able to diagnose a mechanical problem and perform a series of repair steps in a logical, timely way during the training course. But if actual work conditions are noisy and chaotic, those conditions may need to be simulated during training.

Similarly, the materials, tools, and aids that learners use in training must match those available on the job. Conditions during training should increasingly approximate conditions on the job.

## Observation

Observation is a good needs assessment technique in two circumstances. First, it is useful when assessing the need for skill-based training. Second, it is a good technique to use when conducting a program that changes behavior (for example, customer service or giving constructive feedback). Table 7-2 describes more advantages and disadvantages of observation.

This data-collection method involves sitting with and observing star performers, experts, or average performers. More advanced versions of this method include time-and-motion studies and human factors studies—the tools of industrial engineers. In this method, an observer watches the job performer and documents each step that the performer implements in the performance of a task, including movements, the amount of time for each step, and standards for successful performance. Learning professionals can use observation to collect data on current and desired performance.

## Table 7-2. Advantages and Disadvantages of Observation

| Advantages | Disadvantages |
|---|---|
| • It is excellent for assessing training needs for physical or psychomotor skills. | • It is sometimes difficult to identify where a specific task begins and ends. |
| • It creates a step-by-step procedure (algorithm) that can be standardized for all learners, in the form of a flowchart, diagram, graphic, list of steps, or job aid. | • It misses the performer's mental processes in making choices at each step unless accompanied with an interview. |
| • If the observer notes job environment conditions that help or hinder performance, these can be included in the data. | • Some performers may act differently than they would normally simply because they know they are being watched (known as the Hawthorne effect). Interviewing the performer after observation and asking why things were done in a certain way can help control for this effect. |

## Table 7-3. Advantages and Disadvantages of Interviews

| Advantages | Disadvantages |
|---|---|
| • They provide rich detail.<br><br>• Careful structuring of the interview protocol produces consistent data across interviews that can be compared to identify patterns and trends.<br><br>• They can be used to flesh out quantitative data collected in a survey. | • They can be time-consuming because of the volume of data.<br><br>• Interviewees must truly represent the targeted population, or the data will be skewed.<br><br>• The frequency of responses does not get at the reason behind the responses (that is, why the respondents felt a certain way).<br><br>• The interviewer must be careful to record interviewee responses and not interpret them. |

Observations accompanied by interviews can produce tools known as **algorithms**. An algorithm depicts both physical steps or behaviors and the thought processes that support those steps.

## Interviews

WLP professionals can use interviews—one-on-one discussions—to elicit the reactions of interviewees to carefully focused topics. This data-collection method yields subjective and perceptive individual data and illustrative anecdotes. It is most often used to collect data on current performance analysis and learner analysis and is also used to gather business needs information from the client. For advantages and disadvantages of interviews, see Table 7-3.

Learning professionals identify people who can provide information about the business or training need and then interview them. The advantage of this type of interview is the ability to obtain in-depth information about the situation and other people's ideas about how to handle the situation. If the learning professional does end up providing a training program, he or she also has some early commitment because people will have had input in shaping the program. These are a few tips for interviewers:

- Set the interviewees at ease. Begin with general questions and small talk. Slowly move into more specific questions.

- Use open-ended questions to get more detailed and rich data. Use closed-ended questions to control the interview and move on.

- Ask the interviewee to confirm and specify generalized statements and assumptions that he or she makes.

- Take notes. Use a page with interview questions already printed on it (called an *interview protocol*) and make notes for each question. The interviewer should show the interviewee his or her protocol and notes if asked.

- In some instances, audiotaping an interview will enable the interviewer to check back for the interviewee's exact wording when analyzing the data. When choosing to audiotape, ensure the interviewee that the purpose is to identify rich anecdotal phraseology and examples that might be significant for the study and for developing learning activities in the later training design. Tell the interviewee that his or her story will not be individually identified and that the tape will be destroyed after the study is complete. The interviewer must then be sure to do so.

Data-collection interviews can be conducted over the telephone as well. Sometimes this is the only way to get an interview with someone who is difficult to reach. Over the phone, learning professionals can use scripts, job aids, and so forth to conduct the interview without the interviewee knowing. Two disadvantages of telephone interviews include not being able to read the interviewee's body language and not being able to tell whether the interviewee is distracted or doing something else during the interview.

Learning professionals can use interviews to accomplish these goals:

- gather background data at the beginning of analysis or supplement and expand data from instruments and observations

- obtain input from those people who better express their views in person than on written surveys or questionnaires (this input can be used to construct more effective instruments)

- identify causes of problems and possible solutions by encouraging interviewees to reveal their feelings and opinions on these matters

- give participants pride of ownership in the analysis process by inviting them to provide the data for diagnosing training needs

- use interviews to clarify ambiguous or confusing information obtained from documentation or observation.

## Focus Groups

Another approach to data collection is to conduct focus groups. Somewhat like an interview, the designer conducts focus groups to identify key people who can provide information about the need. However, instead of being interviewed individually, they are interviewed in groups. The group interview provides rich data regarding the performers' or learners' job environment, current level of skill and performance, and perceptions of desired skill and performance level. Focus groups can be used to collect information about current performance, learning needs, and learner needs. Advantages and disadvantages of focus groups are listed in Table 7-4.

## Table 7-4. Advantages and Disadvantages of Focus Groups

| Advantages | Disadvantages |
| --- | --- |
| • They develop hypotheses that can be tested with a larger population through surveys or observations.<br><br>• The facilitator can make note of nonverbal behaviors that accompany statements.<br><br>• Skilled facilitation results in all focus group members—not just the more verbal participants—being heard. | • They are time and resource intensive.<br><br>• Sometimes a focus group can fall under the influence of particularly verbal members and give the impression of unanimity when it is not necessarily the case.<br><br>• A focus group is difficult to facilitate with just one facilitator who must run the group and take notes. |

Conducting a focus group on neutral turf is important (for example, in a conference room that is not in the group's work area). When scheduling people to participate, the learning professional needs to be general: "We are going to talk about the challenges of conducting job interviews." Specifying the topic too specifically ahead of time allows participants to prepare canned responses.

The size of a focus group should stay between five and 12 participants. Another option is to implement multiple groups to get segmented data: a group of high performers, a group of average performers, and a group of performers' managers. When facilitating a focus group, the learning professional uses a focus group protocol and moves from general to specific questions. For example, he or she may start with, "How are job interviews conducted at your organization?" and gradually move to more specific questions, such as "In terms of legal or illegal interview questions, what are the trickiest areas, in your opinion?"

The facilitator of the focus group should use questions that encourage the participants to speak up while he or she stays as quiet as possible. The facilitator must not convey via verbal or nonverbal communication agreement or disagreement with any participant statements and avoid interjecting his or her own comments about the subject. To document the data the facilitator may ask someone to take notes on flipcharts or on paper (the facilitator shouldn't do it him- or herself because facilitating the group is enough to do), or consider audiotaping. If the facilitator decides to tape the sessions, he or she should begin by offering assurances regarding anonymity and stating that the tape will be destroyed after it is transcribed.

## Surveys

Surveys are paper-and-pencil or electronic or email questionnaires that ask respondents a series of focused questions. Surveys are most often used for performance analysis and learner analysis for training needs assessment.

# Table 7-5. Advantages and Disadvantages of Surveys

| Advantages | Disadvantages |
|---|---|
| • They are inexpensive. <br><br>• The results are easy to tally.<br><br>• Participation is easy.<br><br>• They provide quick results.<br><br>• Frequencies (how many respondents answered a question each way) are easy to understand.<br><br>• They can be qualitative also: Soft data questions yield qualitative data; the answer tally is quantitative. | • Constructing questions that get the desired data in a configuration that meets the learning professional's needs is challenging. (He or she must be careful with wording.)<br><br>• Ensuring that the wording of a question means the same thing to all respondents (reliability) and that the wording of the question will garner the information that is sought (face validity) is necessary.<br><br>• Choosing an appropriate answer scale is critical.<br><br>• Respondents can skew the results by simply checking all one type of answer without really reading the questions.<br><br>• Getting a large enough sample to make the data reliable can be difficult. |

Surveys vary greatly in the amount of time and money they require and in complexity (more disadvantages as well as advantages are presented in Table 7-5). The learning professional should choose the type of survey that will best provide the needed data—not necessarily the fastest, least expensive, and easiest one to do. Another factor to consider is that more than one type of survey may be needed to obtain different kinds of data about the same topic.

Some useful points for learning professionals to remember when using surveys include

- Surveys can be used to gather both qualitative and quantitative data.

- Surveys help to gather information from employees and managers who have a vested interest in succeeding. Surveys help to gain support from these groups by providing them with an input mechanism—they help employees and management team members understand that the organization wants them to succeed.

- Surveys have various questioning options and rating scales, such as Likert scale, multiple-choice, and forced-choice questions. (More on these and other scales follows.) These can even be combined for cross-referencing of data.

## Likert Scale

The Likert scale is a linear scale used to rate statements and attitudes. Respondents receive a definition of the scale, ranging from 1 to 10 with, for example, 1 indicating least important and 10 indicating most important.

## Semantic Differential

In a survey that uses a semantic differential, participants rate two contrasting ideas or words separated by a graduated line, either numbered or unnumbered. They indicate frequency of behavior or depth of opinion by circling points on the line. An example that measures the value of new equipment follows:

**VALUABLE ————————— USELESS**
**1 2 3 4 5 6 7 8 9 10**

## Alternative Response

Alternative response is an inventory format that forces respondents to choose between two acceptable statements. The choices present a pattern of responses indicating tendencies toward particular behaviors or attitudes. This is the most difficult type of instrument to construct because both statements must be plausible enough to present a difficult choice but sufficiently different to distinguish two separate sets of beliefs and attitudes.

## Multiple-Choice Questions

Multiple-choice questions, which are also difficult to construct, consist of choosing one item or statement from several well-planned and well-written choices. Each choice must be logically consistent with all elements of the instrument. The results indicate a person's style, behavior patterns, and attitudes. For example, with this format identifying and analyzing styles of leadership, communication, training, problem solving, management, and sales are possible.

## Open-Ended Questions

This essay question format also may be difficult to construct. Questions must be objective, free of the questioner's biases, and clear enough for respondents to complete without a great deal of assistance. These questions are not limited to preselected responses.

## Completion

The completion format presents well-designed completion questions that encourage participants to disclose opinions and perceptions about themselves, their jobs and careers, and other workers or managers. Some experts have found that completion helps to focus

## Table 7-6. Advantages and Disadvantages of Work Samples

| Advantages | Disadvantages |
|---|---|
| • This method is unobtrusive.<br><br>• As is the case with records and reports, this method provides clues to trouble spots.<br><br>• This method provides direct data on the organization's actual work. | • Using this method may be costly and time-consuming. The wrong sample will provide little or no information.<br><br>• To use this data-gathering method, the designer's skills must include specialized content skills.<br><br>• Workers may alter their behavior if they know that some kind of observation is in progress. |

and stimulate respondents' thinking, more so than the open-ended format, because it forces them to use their own thoughts and language to complete or fill in the blanks.

## Work Samples

Learning professionals can gather frontline information in the form of tangible work samples, such as the manager's reports, a secretary's typing, a repairperson's mending of equipment, or a computer programmer's new software design. Or work samples can be less tangible, such as an instructor presenting a lesson or a manager conducting a meeting.

WLP professionals use work samples to identify problem areas that may require further analysis. If a department's or an individual's products are found unsatisfactory on a regular basis, an investigation may be necessary. Work samples also may be used to supplement other assessment methods, to validate other data, and to gather preliminary information for the study. Advantages and disadvantages of using work samples are presented in Table 7-6.

## Extant Data (Records and Reports)

Existing records, reports, and data comprise extant data, which may be available inside or outside the organization. Examples include job descriptions, competency models, benchmarking reports, annual reports, financial statements, strategic plans, mission statements, staffing statistics, climate surveys, 360-degree feedback, performance appraisals, grievances, turnover rates, absenteeism, suggestion box feedback, accident statistics, and so forth.

Learning professionals often use extant data for business needs analysis and current performance analysis. Table 7-7 lists some advantages and disadvantages of using extant data for training needs assessment.

## Table 7-7. Advantages and Disadvantages of Extant Data

| Advantages | Disadvantages |
|---|---|
| • It provides hard data and measures.<br><br>• It can enable an examination of trends and patterns in data over time.<br><br>• It has consistent measurements that provide reliable data.<br><br>• It does not involve individual employee confidentiality issues because data is used in aggregate form. | • Extant data is usually collected for purposes other than training needs assessment, so training issues must be inferred from patterns in the data.<br><br>• The learning professional has no control over the methodology used to collect the data.<br><br>• Extant data can be mixed in with data that is extraneous to the purpose, so it must be "sifted." |

Once the learning professional has determined the type of data to collect and the instrument(s) to use, he or she is ready to collect the data. The following are some tips to help learning professionals implement the process efficiently and effectively:

- ***Double check:*** The learning professional should take a last quick pass over his or her choices and the reasons for choosing each method. He or she should not be afraid to make last-minute adjustments before starting. Being sure the selected methods will optimize time, access to resources, and the ultimate value of the data is important.

- ***Make a plan:*** WLP professionals should develop a calendar, timeline, flowchart, or some other tool to help stay on track and provide reminders of deadlines to complete data collection. They should monitor progress on the plan as they go along.

- ***Be flexible:*** One of the advantages of having a plan is that learning professionals know when to deviate from it. Things happen in organizational life that are out of the control of learning professionals, and they should be prepared to adjust their data collection as they go along.

- ***Include the sponsor regularly and frequently:*** The training sponsor must approve the WLP professional's data-collection plan. The learning and performance professional must also report to the sponsor periodically about progress. The report doesn't have to be formal; even a voicemail message or email will do. If the WLP professional stays in touch with the sponsor, if he or she must change the plan due to organizational circumstances, the sponsor will know about it and can help gain access to alternative data sources.

- ***Keep personal interpretations and experiences out of the data collection:*** This is critical. The data must be objective, or the ultimate data analysis will not be accurate.

- *Be objective:* The learning professional must avoid structuring data collection to play on a hunch. For example, if the WLP professional gets a hunch during an initial interview with a sponsor that part of a performance problem is obsolete equipment then asking a question in the interview or survey like "What problems have you had with equipment?" is leading and plays too closely on the hunch. Instead, the question might be "What keeps you from achieving the results that are expected of you?"

- *Use extant data correctly:* Extant data is rarely if ever collected for the learning and performance professional's purposes, so he or she must infer from that data and take steps to validate the inferences if necessary. For example, if the WLP professional hears consistent comments from an exit interview, he or she needs to validate the comments because they might not necessarily be true; employees may only believe them to be true.

## Results of Needs Assessment

The final step in conducting a needs assessment is the opportunity to present the results. By organizing information and discussing interpretations from analysis, the WLP professional can succinctly and clearly convince management that the proposed learning will solve the identified problem or problems and respond to management's request. Communicating the results in writing and in a spoken presentation usually improves chances for success.

The final report defines and documents findings of the needs assessment process and summarizes the problem statement, the analyses used to determine the training need, and a proposed module design. In the final report, the learning professional discusses how the findings relate to the organization's overall strategy and goals and how the proposed change or training program will benefit the organization and the employees.

The results of needs assessments should include

- the organization's goals and its effectiveness in reaching those goals
- discrepancies between current and future performance
- a determination of root causes of suboptimal performance level
- a determination of whether a training requirement exists
- types of programs needed
- conditions under which learning will occur
- the target audience for the program
- a determination of desired performance (training results)
- baseline data
- content and scope of training
- participant and organizational support that involves appropriate SMEs, sponsors, and other vested stakeholders early in the process.

## ✓ Chapter 7 Knowledge Check

1. **Which of the following best describes training needs assessment, which is often also referred to as training needs analysis?**

   ___ A. Training needs assessment is the process of collecting and synthesizing data to identify training requirements.

   ___ B. Training needs assessment identifies the discrepancy between the desired and actual knowledge, skills, and performance and specifies root causes.

   ___ C. Training needs assessment identifies all duties and responsibilities and the respective tasks done on a daily, weekly, monthly, or yearly basis.

   ___ D. Training needs assessment is the process of identifying the specific steps to correctly perform a job function.

2. **All of the following are benefits of conducting a needs assessment *except***

   ___ A. Identifying performance problems, deficiencies, and the root causes

   ___ B. Determining whether training is the best solution to problems

   ___ C. Training managers to train content to their department personnel

   ___ D. Justifying spending to top management

3. **All of the following are steps in conducting a training needs assessment *except***

   ___ A. Defining the objectives

   ___ B. Selecting the data collection method

   ___ C. Selecting learning strategies

   ___ D. Identifying the required data

4. **Which of the following is one way that an organization can find out what kind of training and development should be promoted?**

   ___ A. Conduct a needs assessment

   ___ B. Develop a strategic plan for the organization

   ___ C. Formalize the training department's instructional design model

   ___ D. Ask managers what training their departments need

**5. Which of the following is an advantage of using interviews as a data-gathering technique?**

___ A. Interviewers can receive additional information in the form of nonverbal messages. Interviewees' behaviors—their gestures, eye contact, and general reactions to questions—are additional data or cues for the next questions.

___ B. This method is unobtrusive.

___ C. This method gives observers an idea of a typical workday and provides a realistic view of the situation.

___ D. Interviews provide direct data on the organization's actual work.

**6. Which of the following instruments has participants rate two contrasting ideas or words that are separated by a graduated line, either numbered or unnumbered? They indicate frequency of behavior or depth of opinion by circling points on the line.**

___ A. Likert scale

___ B. Semantic differential

___ C. Alternative choice

___ D. Completion

**7. Designers should rely primarily on one data-gathering technique to ensure consistency and accuracy of results.**

___ A. True

___ B. False

**8. Which of the following is used to identify the efficiency and effectiveness of employees?**

___ A. Performance audit

___ B. Competency modeling

___ C. Interviews

___ D. Observation

**9. Quantitative methods of collecting data are those that result in**

___ A. Valid data

___ B. Soft data

___ C. Hard data

___ D. Extant data

# References

Biech, E. (2005). *Training for Dummies*®. Hoboken, NJ: Wiley Publishing.

Long, L. (1986). "Surveys From Start to Finish." *Infoline* No. 258612.

McArdle, G.E. (1999). *Training Design and Delivery*. Alexandria, VA: ASTD Press.

Piskurich, G., P. Beckschi, and B. Hall, eds. (2000). *The ASTD Handbook of Training Design and Delivery*. New York: McGraw-Hill.

Sharpe, C., ed. (1997). "Be a Better Needs Analyst." *Infoline* No. 258502.

Sparhawk, S., and M. Schickling. (1994). "Strategic Needs Analysis." *Infoline* No. 259408.

Tobey, D. (2005). *Needs Assessment Basics*. Alexandria, VA: ASTD Press.

Waagen, A.K. (1998). "Task Analysis." *Infoline* No. 259808.

# 8
# Learning Technologies and Support Systems

 Technology is changing the way learning occurs within organizations on a daily basis. Understanding the different technologies available and their use within a particular organization is critical to providing value-driven training and learning. Because technology can either be a hindrance or an enhancement to learning, a WLP professional needs to understand what the technology can do and should know its advantages and disadvantages.

Developments in the web have created revolutionary changes in the ways that training and development groups offer instruction and information to their organizations' employees. Training and performance support via the web is only one of the many technology-mediated learning applications collectively called ***e-learning*** or ***learning technologies***. Other technology-based training applications, such as CD-ROMs and computer-based training (CBT), may be more familiar to trainers and developers.

Learning information systems not only support the work efforts of WLP professionals but also strengthen the organization. They can facilitate the learning process by supporting the processes of knowledge acquisition, information distribution, information interpretation, and organizational memory. With the displacement of people due to downsizing efforts, organizations are discharging vast amounts of organizational knowledge without realizing the long-term implications of such short-term actions. The only way organizations can preserve the knowledge and further promote organizational learning is to use information systems to store and retrieve such collective knowledge.

A learning information system is one of the tools that benefits the training manager on several levels: program administration and design and delivery of training. At the administration level, learning information systems provide databases for administering training programs, which generates rosters, certificates, and registration reports. They can also store templates and modules of information for building training curricula. They can also be used at the learner level in the classroom, through e-learning, and with self-paced materials, reference documents, and job aids.

## Learning Objective:

☑ Define the key differences in various learning technologies and support systems, including learning management systems.

# Key Knowledge: Learning Information Systems

A training manager can implement many learning systems to support the training function; learner needs; and content design, development, and delivery. This section provides an overview of four types of learning information systems as summarized by Greenberg (2002) and Hall and Hall (2004):

- learning management systems (LMSs)

- learning content management systems (LCMSs)

- collaborative learning software

- learning support systems (LSSs).

It's difficult for buyers to determine whether it's best to purchase an LMS, an LCMS, or both and what type of collaborative learning software should be implemented to support all training and learner needs. This confusion is partly due to the fact that many buyers fail to grasp the distinctions between LMSs and LCMSs and the types of collaborative learning software that may already be included with those systems. Although many vendors offer combination LCMS-LMS systems, there are core differences between the two. An LCMS manages content (the components that make up a course), while an LMS manages learners (who's taking what, completion ratios, course progress status, scheduling, and so on).

LCMSs put together the most essential pieces of the learning puzzle—namely, courses and learning materials. LCMSs package content for print, CD-ROM, or electronic publication, and most are capable of importing prepackaged content from other learning content development tools, such as Microsoft Word and Macromedia Dreamweaver.

In addition to using LCMSs for managing and packaging content, course developers can also often use them as a primary authoring tool for developing learning content. It's important to note that an LCMS's ability to cleanly import content from various sources is crucial in learning organizations.

Collaborative technologies (also called collaborative learning software) have emerged to offer a way to familiarize learners with new expectations and experiences. Collaboration tools include email, computer networks, whiteboards, bulletin board systems, chat rooms, and online presentation tools. These technologies play a significant role in the expansion of e-learning as well as in collaboration on projects, the sharing of information, and communication.

For more information, see Module 6, *Managing the Learning Function*, Chapters 4 and 5, "Learning Technologies" and "Learning Information Systems."

# 9
# New and Emerging Learning Technologies

 Technology improvements and new products come on the market continually. The role of a WLP professional includes keeping up with these changes and being able to evaluate these technologies in light of the learning goals established by the organization and changes within the industry. So what are learning technologies? When combined in the phrase "learning technologies," the words become a concept that many trainers define in different ways. For the purposes of this publication, learning technologies are defined as electronic technologies that deliver information and facilitate the development of skills and knowledge.

Examining the learning products that result from technology improvements is important, but so is understanding the effects product specifications might have. WLP professionals must learn to take time out from pressures of the status quo and reactive solutions to incoming requests and look to the future and emerging learning technologies that they need to plan for or leverage. To truly add value to their organizations, they need to provide current or updated programs, use appropriate technology for delivery and communication, understand the current business climate and anticipated changes, and respond to changing workforce demographics and future training needs.

According to *The 2005 ASTD State of the Industry Report*, use of technology for delivering learning continued to increase, from 24 percent in 2003 to 27 percent in 2004 in benchmarking survey organizations and from 35 percent to 38 percent in benchmarking forum organizations. BEST Awards organizations delivered 32 percent of all its learning content using technology. Approximately 75 percent of technology-based learning was online in 2004, and about 75 percent of online learning was self-paced.

## Learning Objectives:

☑ Describe why WLP professionals need to stay abreast of emerging trends.

☑ List three resources for keeping current with regard to learning technologies and support systems.

## Key Knowledge: Emerging Learning Technologies

It takes a team to implement learning technologies. WLP professionals must understand that they can't implement learning technologies effectively on their own. Even a large staff probably won't possess all the technical expertise necessary for implementing these technologies, which change rapidly and have many specifications for a trainer or training manager to try to handle alone.

Instead, partnerships with members of the technical community (for example, information systems professionals, information technology professionals, and so forth) are necessary to make these learning technologies efficient and effective.

When implementing and evaluating new learning technologies, there are many layers of responsibility. For example, responsibilities of designers, developers, and implementers are different from the responsibilities of managers, evaluators, analysts, and organizational change agents. Each role deals with information that's on a very different plane.

Decisions about technology selection made by the human resource manager involve a detailed understanding of the organization's goals, the existing technology infrastructure, budgetary requirements, and external forces. For the designer, the considerations are more pragmatic. Designers, knowing which distribution technologies are available, focus on how to make the most of these available resources. This focus requires careful consideration of how they can pair each instructional method, presentation method, and available distribution method to create effective learning experiences.

The evaluator, analyst, and organizational change agent's considerations center on the amount of change these learning solutions are likely to produce. Only through careful measurement can WLP professionals determine what effect this training had on the organization.

So how can trainers and training managers keep current on emerging learning technologies? Professional development groups and organizations, such as the American Society for Training & Development (ASTD), the International Society for Performance Improvement (ISPI), information technology organizations, and the Society for Human Resource Management (SHRM), provide training to assist WLP professionals on keeping current in the industry and with emerging technologies. For practitioners in this industry, lifelong learning is a given.

For more information, see Module 6, *Managing the Learning Function*, Chapter 16, "Emerging Learning Technologies."

# 10
# Business Strategy and Drivers

 An effective WLP professional strives to be aware of the context of the learning being designed, such as how the learning is connected to the overall business strategy, the environment in which the learning will occur, or the goals and perspectives of key stakeholders in the project. Designers balance the qualities of the most elegant learning solution with the needs of the business to propose solutions that work as effectively as possible within business constraints.

A WLP professional needs to have a basic understanding of how businesses function in an organization's particular community, how funding and revenues are determined, and what are the strategic strengths and weaknesses of the business. A learning professional must be able to convey learning initiatives in the terminology of his or her organization so that the function is seen as a strategic business partner. To become a strategic partner, WLP practitioners should focus on

- providing services that support the organization's business strategy
- improving the visibility of his or her activities and accomplishments to gain credibility for the learning function
- measuring results or at least tying results to other internal measures
- becoming educated in strategic planning
- educating others in the strategic planning process.

## Learning Objective:

☑ Describe the importance of understanding the business drivers and needs that gave rise to an identified need prior to designing the instruction.

## Key Knowledge: Business Drivers and Needs

The learning function cannot be a valued business partner if the practitioner does not understand the business model, business objectives, growth factors, and strategic drivers for an organization and its industry. In completing this analysis, a practitioner also needs to understand corporate "measures of success" and how the organization defines and measures success. These factors will all drive how the training programs in the organization are created and linked to the business goals and objectives.

Once the practitioner has defined the big-picture perspective regarding the state of the industry, goals, and objectives, and how success is measured in the organization, he or she should examine the company culture and value systems. The culture of an organization—the assumptions shared by employees about their work and their feelings toward the organization—cannot be ignored during the analysis. An assessment of the culture and the degree to which it helps or hinders deployment of a strategic plan is critical to the success of the plan.

Continual environmental scanning must be institutionalized to proactively assess the effect of change on an organization. A strengths, weaknesses, opportunities, and threats (SWOT) analysis, based on changes in the environmental trends and forces—both current and future—should be performed as strengths and weaknesses shift and when new opportunities or threats are uncovered by the assessment.

To understand the learning function role in a business, WLP professionals must know the organizational structure in which they function and how it operates to accomplish company objectives. Practitioners need to understand the type of organizational structure (for example, line, staff, committee, functional, or matrix) and the advantages and disadvantages of each.

These structures help to define department functions; roles and responsibilities; relationships between departments; reporting structures; organizational layout—meaning with whom does the employee exchange information, documents, and other resources to perform his or her role—and the workflow network or formal organizational structure supporting the workflow for business processes and how each process works.

Knowledge exchanges can also be a competitive advantage by enabling different groups within an organization to share documents and information on products, create lists of links within simple webpages, and discuss issues of mutual interest, which facilitate knowledge management in an organization.

For more information, see Module 6, *Managing the Learning Function*, Chapter 13, "Business Model, Drivers, and Competitive Position."

# 11
# Research Methods

 WLP professionals need to know how to design research methods to be able to implement measurement and evaluation activities, assess proposed methods, and make recommendations on how to implement a measurement and evaluation activity. Expertise in this knowledge area benefits a WLP professional by providing the foundation for implementing measurement and evaluation activities and is part of the instructional design phases of analysis and evaluation.

One of the biggest challenges when embarking on an organizational evaluation strategy is determining which results to measure and how to measure them. A measure is a standard used to assess the results of a performance solution. It is essential to the evaluation to select measures before designing and developing the program.

The most important step in establishing measures for an evaluation is to validate the business drivers (Barksdale and Lund 1998). Business drivers are the internal and external forces that direct an organization's strategy, goals, business needs, and performance needs. External business drivers can include economics, human resources, government, public perception, and market or customer drivers. Internal business drivers are generated by internal decisions and can include technology; a change in system, process, or key policy; shareholder or financial drivers; and new product generation.

Once the business drivers and performance needs have been identified, the measurement approach can be determined. This measurement approach is centered most often on the level of Kirkpatrick's evaluation model that will be followed, but other models may be used as well. It is feasible to have three to five measures and corresponding approaches for the evaluation strategy. When considering specific evaluation approaches, a key discussion point should be to determine how the specific learning approach rolls into the evaluation strategy measures.

The specific data for the training should fit under the evaluation strategy umbrella. If it has a completely different parameter that does not fit, it is important to ask why and to determine if the evaluation strategy may be missing an important factor or if something else has changed in the environment and strategy maintenance is called for.

## Learning Objective:

☑ Explain the importance of research planning and knowledge of assessment techniques to design data-gathering plans.

## Key Knowledge: Research Design

Research design for measuring and evaluating training and development is critical to the success of the evaluation. The following describes several major concepts related to research design:

*Dependent, independent, and extraneous variables:* An *independent variable* is controlled by the evaluator and is the influencing variable. *Dependent variables* are the influenced variables. *Extraneous variables* are undesirable variables that influence the relationship between the variables an evaluator is examining.

*Research questions:* Research questions can appear in many different formats. Wording in questionnaires is extremely important, because the success of a questionnaire depends on words alone. Questions that are open for interpretation may invalidate months of hard work.

*Experimental design process:* This is the proper organization of a research project to ensure that the right type of data, and enough of it, is available to answer the questions of interest as clearly and efficiently as possible. Practitioners should clearly identify the specific questions that a research project is intended to answer before carrying out the project.

*Statistical and design control of variables:* A *control group* is a group of participants in an experiment that is equal in all ways to the experimental group except for having received the experimental treatment. A factor of an experiment is a controlled independent variable, a variable whose levels are set by the evaluator.

*Qualitative research:* Data-collection methods are either qualitative or quantitative. Quantitative methods are those that result in hard data, whereas qualitative measures yield soft data.

*Sampling:* In simple terms, a *sample* is a portion of the population that an evaluator is interested in collecting data on. A sample should be a cross-section of the population, with all the characteristics of the population represented.

For more information, see Module 4, *Measuring and Evaluating Training*, Chapter 3, "Research Design."

# 12
# Individual and Organizational Influences on Learning

 Change may be a business decision, but during transition there are significant emotional and political effects on the organization's people, the human capital asset, to consider. Understanding what motivates employees varies by generation; however, understanding motivating factors is perhaps the most critical element to consider while implementing organizational change.

The effect could be resistance, turnover, and failure to institutionalize the change. Failure to maximize retention during the time of major change can also affect the quality of the change initiative outcome (result). Having change agents involved during the planning stage of the initiative can minimize potential issues on the front lines closest to the customers. These agents, strategically placed at all levels, can become SMEs and minimize the effects of "lightning rods" against the change.

Understanding how others are motivated can help a manager harness the potentially threatening resistance by some and transform them into allies who stand as part of the solution. Empowering employees to make choices can help ensure the change is institutionalized. Management can contribute directly to motivation during this transition by rewarding those who have embraced the change and providing additional support for those who have not.

Motivating employees to achieve their potential is one of the most difficult challenges facing any manager or supervisor. The training of managers and supervisors in employee motivation involves giving them the background they need to understand what motivation is and how to tap this drive among their employees.

Motivation is classically defined as the desire to work: the amount of effort put forth on a job. Every person has a mindset that determines how and why he or she behaves in a certain manner. These activities are based on motivational factors, such as personal goals, organizational and personal reward systems, and job enrichment.

## Learning Objective:

☑ Identify individual and social factors that influence an adult's learning capacity.

## Key Knowledge: Employee Motivation

In today's business climate, rewards and recognition have become more important than ever. Many managers, however, think that the only thing that motivates employees is money. Motivational experts agree that money is *not* the best way to motivate employees, yet, according to management specialist and author Bob Nelson, "It is a rare manager who systematically makes the effort simply to thank employees for a job well done, let alone to do something more innovative to recognize accomplishments."

When examining the workplace environment, WLP professionals may discover two influences that have great effect on the motivation of employees: management and performance. Instead of coming from some nebulous ad hoc committee or corporate institution, the most valuable recognition comes directly from one's manager. Employees want to be recognized for the jobs they were hired to do. The most effective incentives are based on job performance—not on nonperformance-related praise, such as attendance or attire.

These influences should be considered when integrating motivation into job design, performance feedback, pay-for-performance systems, and relationship-building initiatives.

Although money, according to Bob Nelson, author of *1001 Ways to Reward Employees,* is important to employees, what tends to motivate them to perform—and to perform at higher levels—"is the thoughtful, personal kind of recognition that signifies true appreciation for a job well done." Examples of this type of recognition include

- buying an employee lunch as a form of thanks or to mark a special event
- greeting employees by name
- engraving a plaque with the names of employees who have served five, 10, and 20 years
- giving the person more autonomy
- paying membership dues for a professional association
- creating symbols of a team's work, such as t-shirts or coffee mugs with a motto or logo
- giving higher-performing employees the chance to telecommute.

Most organizations boast of their goals for employee development and growth. Managers, supervisors, and employees need to discuss and agree on the methods that will be used before development and growth will occur.For more information, see Module 5, *Facilitating Organizational Change*, Chapter 11, "Motivation Theory."

# 13
# Legal and Ethical Issues

 Training professionals must get permission and give credit appropriately when using materials as part of a class—and should also ensure that participants are aware of and understand these guidelines. Materials shared during a training session might be in print or electronic format and may be confidential.

The WLP professional must be aware of legislative initiatives that affect the organization's strategic vision and employees. One of the most important laws is copyright. Using a work that's protected by copyright for training purposes requires permission from the copyright owner. Trainers must understand how laws and regulations may affect the design, delivery, and measurement of a learning or performance initiative.

Title 17, Code of Federal Regulations, Section 107. Limitations on exclusive rights states that " . . . the fair use of a copyrighted work, including such use by reproduction in copies or phonorecords or by any other means specified by that section, for purposes such as criticism, comment, news reporting, teaching (including multiple copies for classroom use), scholarship, or research, is not an infringement of copyright.

In determining whether the use made of a work in any particular case is a fair use, the factors to be considered shall include

"(1) the purpose and character of the use, including whether such use is of a commercial nature or is for nonprofit educational purposes

"(2) the nature of the copyrighted work

"(3) the amount and substantiality of the portion used in relation to the copyrighted work as a whole

"(4) the effect of the use upon the potential market for or value of the copyrighted work."

"The fact that a work is unpublished shall not bar a finding of fair use if such finding is made upon consideration of all the above factors" (As amended 1990).

Title 17, Code of Federal Regulations Section 201, continues "(b) Works Made For Hire. In the case of a work made for hire, the employer or other person for whom the work made for hire, the employer or other person for whom the work was prepared is considered the author for [purposes of Title 17], unless the parties have agreed expressly otherwise in a written instrument signed by them, owns all of the rights comprised in the copyright" (As amended 1976).

## Learning Objective:

☑ Explain the importance of legal and ethical issues related to designing learning.

## Key Knowledge: Legal and Ethical Issues

The copyright law protects the expression of ideas (but not the idea itself) in some tangible form (such as book, magazine, video or film, microfilm, cassette tape, computer disk, and so on). Although the exact words in a book may be copyrighted, the ideas in the book are not.

The following can't be copyrighted: ideas, processes, procedures, methods of operation, concepts, principles, or discoveries. However, a tangible description, explanation, or illustration of these may be copyrighted.

A copyright is secured immediately and automatically when the work is created, and a work is created when it's fixed in some form of a tangible expression (such as a computer disk or print copy). Registering the work with the U.S. Copyright Office provides legal protection and redress in state and federal courts.

A copyright holder has the exclusive right to

- reproduce the copyrighted work

- prepare derivative works (adaptation) based on the copyrighted work

- distribute copies of the copyrighted work to the public by sale or other transfer of ownership, or by rental, lease, or lending

- perform the copyrighted work publicly, in the case of motion pictures or other audiovisual works

- display the copyrighted work publicly, in the case of audiovisual work.

Exclusive rights are qualified by the fair use privilege, which allows others to use copyrighted material in a reasonable manner without consent. Although legal guidelines exist, fair use is a tricky legal concept to understand.

In fair use, an author is free to copy from a protected work for purposes of criticism, news reporting, teaching, or research as long as the value of the copyrighted work isn't diminished for the author. Proper citations should always be used to avoid passing the work off as original (an act known as plagiarism). The best practice is to obtain written consent from the copyright holder to use the materials, even for an educational program. However, protection is available to use materials in a training context; despite that, making sure all citations or other attribution to copyrighted work are included is prudent.

For more information, see Module 6, *Managing the Learning Function,* Chapter 15, "Legal, Regulatory, and Ethical Requirements."

# 14
# E-Learning Versus Traditional Courses

E-learning or web-based courses are becoming more commonplace in the adult education market. The WLP professional must be able to identify how this technology evolution affects his or her work and apply the concepts of adult learning and instructional systems development.

Just as adult learning theories affect the design of conventional training, they also have a role to play in designing web-based training in terms of relating the design of the materials to the differences in the way adults learn; ensuring that web-based programs will engage learners; explaining why web-based training is designed as it is; outlining how learning theory influences knowledge, acquisition, retention, and application of information; and linking learning theory with knowledge management.

## Learning Objectives:

- ☑ List three advantages and disadvantages of asynchronous web-based training.

- ☑ Discuss three advantages of classroom learning.

- ☑ Discuss when e-learning might be a better design than classroom learning.

# Comparison of Classroom Training and E-Learning

Now more than ever, the training needs of organizations extend beyond classroom instruction. Conventional classroom-based training often is unable to provide the continuous, individualized learning and performance improvement that electronic media, such as the web, can offer. This situation exists because, in many cases, conventional training is not developed proactively to meet a company's strategic business needs. Rather, it has been implemented in a reactive mode, in response to a performance deficiency or a request.

An example of this kind of training is product training designed as a remedy for a perceived lack of knowledge. Such training might involve, for example, salespeople or customer service representatives learning facts about products and completing a set of tasks using the new information. Learning professionals also can use e-learning or web-based training (WBT) in that way—simply to address performance deficiencies. However, e-learning also enables learners proactively to seek out instantly available resources, when and where the learners need them.

To continue with the example of product training, learning professionals can structure e-learning to mirror the offerings of conventional classroom training (for example, an introduction to new information, opportunities for practice, and testing). But it offers trainees much more, for example, instant access to a vast array of electronic resources, such as databases and competitors' product information (prices, marketing materials, instructors, or field professionals). Those resources can be incorporated item-by-item into the training, in accordance with individual learner needs.

A related problem with conventional training is that offering continuous learning opportunities is difficult in traditional formats where learning is formalized and scheduled with specific beginning and ending times. Because of access limitations, learning may be viewed as a one-shot opportunity or a biannual event. E-learning, however, provides learners with continuous learning opportunities. Learning can take place 15 minutes every day if that schedule suits learner's continuous learning and training needs. Continuous learning can be crucial in business environments in which the pace of change is rapid.

Conventional classroom-based training requires physical presence, a requirement that can be costly in terms of both travel expenses and lost time spent traveling. Even if travel is not required, employees who work at a distance from the office may be denied training opportunities. Distance learning and CBT address the needs of distance learners. WBT brings them even closer, with the added functionality and stimulation of real-time online communication and instant information.

A final deficiency of conventional training is the difficulty in integrating such training with performance support. Although they are related, training and performance support are not the same thing. As a practice, training targets specific knowledge, skills, or competencies; performance support tries to improve how workers do their jobs by taking into account a wider range of factors that influence performance. Such solutions often include training, but they can also focus on nontraining organizational influences, such as access to information on the job, the work environment, or the usability of job aids.

The gap between training and performance may be wider in conventional training than in e-learning, rendering the training less effective, or less relevant than it could be. For example, the information in conventional training materials may quickly become outdated, and those materials thus become ineffective as performance support tools. Also, paper-based training materials, such as a binder with worksheets and tables, are unwieldy tools compared with an online program that, for example, teaches trainees how to identify potential customers through web-based research. E-learning can operate easily as a performance support tool because of the adaptability and flexibility of its content and structure. Therefore, e-learning can integrate training and performance support seamlessly to an extent nearly impossible with conventional training.

Despite its benefits, e-learning may not always be the most efficient or effective approach to training and performance improvement. In some cases, continuing to use only conventional training or creating a blended program that combines conventional and e-learning may make sense. Being capable of assessing the benefits and drawbacks of e-learning within the organizational context (especially if asked to justify the costs associated with the initial implementation of such training) is a vital skill for learning and performance professionals.

# Advantages of E-Learning

E-learning has several key advantages. It

- addresses learning at the individual level
- can be designed for use anytime and anywhere (provided access to a computer)
- maximizes connections among learner(s) and resources
- can be designed to be learner-driven at a pace that corresponds with an individual's learning style
- can be used at the learner's job site, as time is available
- makes it possible to access resources quickly and easily at any time through online search engines
- does not require additional physical space
- connects learners in diverse locations
- enables immediate implementation of new learning
- facilitates seamless connection between training and performance support.

*Asynchronous e-learning* refers to an e-learning environment that does not require the trainer and the learner to participate at the same time. Examples are self-paced courses taken over the Internet or with a CD-ROM, online discussion groups, and email. Advantages of asynchronous e-learning include

- greater flexibility for participants
- greater opportunity for reflection prior to feedback
- practical application time between sessions
- increased interaction among learners through email, chats, and so forth
- opportunity for all participants to communicate full thoughts
- reduced costs, higher return-on-investment (ROI).

## Disadvantages of E-Learning

Despite e-learning's many benefits, several potential drawbacks must be considered before an implementation decision is made.

- Learners may feel that e-learning is less personal.
- E-learning requires excellent instructional design and production.
- Long lead time is required for development between needs identification and delivery.
- Technical requirements may be hard to meet by the organization and individuals:
  - Online activity may be time-consuming with regard to potential response time because of a high volume of Internet traffic or bandwidth issues.
  - Additional software may be needed, such as plug-ins and extensions, which can complicate both development and use of the program, especially if the learner has to take extra time or needs assistance in downloading them.
- Initial implementation of an e-learning program can be expensive, even prohibitively so for some organizations. In the short term, conventional training costs less. If the need for training is not strong across the organization, implementing an expensive e-learning program may not be a good idea.
- Learners may feel disenfranchised if an electronic form of training entirely replaces traditional classroom-based training. Especially if they are mobile workers, that feeling can lead to decreased productivity, morale problems, and higher turnover.

### Is E-Learning the Answer?

To determine if e-learning is an appropriate solution, the WLP professional should consider these questions before committing resources to development:

- What is the nature of the performance deficiency or the learning opportunity that the intended program is expected to address? What are some of the attributes of the targeted deficiencies or opportunities?

- Is instruction or training the most appropriate solution to achieve anticipated results? Would a performance support solution work just as well or better than instruction or training? Are both required? Is the core of the performance problem related to a need to build knowledge, skills, and competencies among the targeted audience? Is the real need related to information access?

- To what degree can technology respond to the identified deficiencies or opportunities? To what degree can it be used in lieu of existing methods of supporting organizational performance improvement?

- Who is the target audience? Are they site-bound or mobile? If site-bound, are they at a single location or campus, or are they dispersed across multiple locations?

- Every project has a budget. Is this one fixed or flexible? In other words, if increasing the project budget to include interactive technology could ultimately save or make more money for the organization, could additional funds be made available to support the project?

- Is interactive technology currently available in this setting? How widespread is it?

- If interactive technology is available, what kinds of resources are available to users currently? Which resources are planned?

- Are those resources developed by commercial vendors? Are they developed by a custom design firm? Are they developed internally? To what kinds of standards or protocols do they adhere?

## Advantages of Classroom Learning

When determining whether to use e-learning or a classroom instruction, the WLP professional should compare the advantages of asynchronous e-learning with the advantages of classroom learning and consider the context of the learning, the needs of adult learners, the needs of the content, and other factors related to instructional design. Advantages of classroom learning include

- face-to-face interaction with an instructor

- addresses learning in a group context

- greater appropriateness for some subjects, for example, motor skills and soft skills

- greater comfort level for some learners who may be more familiar with a traditional training environment

- the ability of learners to communicate emotions and instructors to gauge participant reactions (body language) and motivate learners

- the ability of the instructor to facilitate and lead others to asking the right questions during discussions to help synthesize new solutions.

## Disadvantages of Classroom Learning

Like e-learning, classroom instruction also has a number of drawbacks to consider. Classroom-based training

- must be scheduled for a time and a location

- may be limited by resources physically present

- moves at a pace set by the group

- may require travel and time away from the learner's regular schedule

- is tied to the classroom setting or to predetermined, prepared materials

- requires physical space

- addresses only participants that are in the same physical space

- can be overridden by crises at hand

- is more likely to cause training and performance support to be approached as separate efforts.

## Blended Learning

Blended learning describes the practice of using several media in one curriculum. It typically refers to the combination of classroom instruction and any type of training that includes self-directed use of online capabilities. It combines the advantages of classroom training with those of e-learning. These are just some of the ways that these advantages combine:

- Because instructors must focus classroom courses on the typical learner, they can rarely meet the needs of individual learners. To address this limitation, instructors can develop course websites with remedial material to give slow learners additional opportunities to master the content.

- For learners who need to adapt the material to specific needs or want to continue with the material, instructors can use a website for enrichment material.

- Some online learners have difficulty with the material, even though it might have been tested extensively with prospective learners. Others need gentle reminders to motivate them to complete courses. Using classroom training or coaching can address these difficulties.

# E-Learning Implementation and Evaluation Considerations

Most e-learning implementations result in the following:

- Evaluation of the learner's ability to meet learning objectives.

- Evaluation of the program design by facilitators.

- Review of implementation-specific elements, such as format.

- Modification of design and materials as suggested by the evaluation.

WLP professionals should create a release plan that states how the training will be delivered, when the training will be available, where the training should not be accessible from (restrictions, like operating systems that are unsupported), and what content should be released to the learners. This document is extremely important, especially when an outside delivery supplier is involved. A release plan will guide the system and improve content dissemination. The release plan should be shared with learners attending the instruction as well as with individuals responsible for the administration of training.

Evaluation for web-based training uses the four levels of conventional training evaluation developed by Donald Kirkpatrick. While the evaluation element of the ADDIE model appears to be the last function, in reality evaluation takes place at every point in the process. In fact, every action in the ISD process has an equal and counterbalancing evaluation element associated with it. Evaluations are conducted at the beginning, middle, end, and sometimes after training. Evaluations are conducted for several reasons, including showing retention, ensuring customer satisfaction, and measuring ROI. These are the four levels of evaluation as defined by Kirkpatrick:

- *Level 1: Reaction* measures how the learner feels or reacts to the training; it is a form of a customer satisfaction survey.

- *Level 2: Learning* measures how the learner improves in KSAs from the beginning to the end of the instruction.

- *Level 3: Behavior* measures how the learner improves in performance back on the job.

- *Level 4: Results* measures the effect of the learning learners acquire on business measures.

In the *analysis* phase, evaluation usually consists of the following:

- review of all research data by SMEs and the design team

- survey, focus group, or other analytical method to validate population, delivery system, course design, and other important training components

- evaluation of resources and constraints data based on reviews by key decision makers

- review of process issues such as deadlines and deliverables.

During the ***design*** phase, evaluation usually is done on the following:

- objectives and evaluation tasks

- materials and media plans

- process issues associated with deadlines and deliverables.

***Development*** phase evaluations include the following:

- full course reviews based on evaluations of learners and facilitators

- review of deadlines and deliverables based on targets set in the design element.

Regardless of whether instruction is provided via e-learning or classroom training, WLP professional should follow an ISD process and ensure that learners have the knowledge and skills needed to accomplish the learning objectives at the end of the instruction.

## ✓ Chapter 14 Knowledge Check

1. **Which of the following is an advantage of asynchronous web-based training?**

   \_\_ A.   Addresses learning in a group context

   \_\_ B.   Ability of learners to communicate emotions in a safe environment

   \_\_ C.   Greater flexibility for participants

   \_\_ D.   Most appropriate for training soft skills

2. **Which of the following is a disadvantage of asynchronous web-based training?**

   \_\_ A.   Requires excellent instructional design and production

   \_\_ B.   Requires physical space

   \_\_ C.   Is more likely to cause training and performance support to be approached as separate efforts

   \_\_ D.   Moves at a pace set by the group

3. **A WLP professional has decided to design an asynchronous web-based program to provide ongoing performance support among the field sales staff. Is the selection of asynchronous web-based training appropriate and why?**

   \_\_ A.   Yes, because this training approach will allow learners to access the training as needed

   \_\_ B.   Yes, because this training approach addresses learning in a group context

   \_\_ C.   No, because of the long lead time needed to develop this type of training

   \_\_ D.   No, because salespeople require a more personal training approach

4. **A WLP professional has decided to design a class to provide ongoing performance support among the field sales staff. Is the selection of classroom training appropriate and why?**

   \_\_ A.   Yes, because this training approach will allow learners to communicate emotions and the instructor to gauge participant reactions

   \_\_ B.   Yes, because this training approach addresses learning in a group context

   \_\_ C.   No, because of the long lead time needed to develop this type of training

   \_\_ D.   No, because this training approach often causes training and performance support to be approached as separate efforts

**5.   Which of the following is an advantage of classroom learning?**

__ A.   Some learners may be more comfortable with classroom training because they may be more familiar with a traditional training environment.

__ B.   Classroom training provides greater flexibility for participants.

__ C.   Learners may have to take time out of their regular schedules to attend training.

__ D.   Classroom training allows for training and performance support to be approached as separate efforts.

# References

Biech, E. (2005). *Training for Dummies®*. Hoboken, NJ: Wiley Publishing.

Ellis, A.L., E.D. Wagner, and W.R. Longmire. (1999). *Managing Web-Based Training*. Alexandria, VA: ASTD Press.

# 15
# Information Displays and Resources

 In addition to the many decisions related to content, course design, and delivery, the WLP professional must also know various ways to access and display information. Learners process information more efficiently when it is displayed appropriately. Learners must also have good access to additional resources, which should be provided in such a way to meet course content requirements and learner needs.

An important role of a WLP professional in the interpretation and reporting of data is converting the data so that it is easy for the general reader to understand. The process begins with selecting data and results to report. Translating data and results into an appropriate format for the intended audience may include ensuring that the chosen graphical format accurately conveys the information and providing supporting contextual material to place data and results in the proper context.

Qualitative data is information that can be difficult to express in measures or numbers. Qualitative analysis involves looking at the opinions, behaviors, and attributes of the participant, and is very often descriptive. The data is typically collected through focus groups and interviews, although it can also come from other sources, such as observer notes and survey comment areas. Often, personal perspectives and direct quotations are noted, and these can be quite wordy.

After the responses are collected, the results need to be tabulated and analyzed. Charts and graphs can be used to summarize the results of each question at a glance. Cross-tab tables can help analyze cause-and-effect and complementary relationships.

The primary tools used for quantitative evaluation are charts and graphs. When displaying this type of information, two guiding principles include scaling and integrity. Scaling shows proportions and relationships. Integrity focuses on the truthfulness and accuracy of the presentation.

## Learning Objective:

☑ Discuss the importance of displays, access, and resources when designing instruction.

# Key Knowledge: Design of Information Displays

Some data-collection instruments have various sources of error inherent in the data received. For example, with telephone surveys and written questionnaires, there can be incomplete surveys and responses. An evaluator needs to decide what constitutes a completed survey; for example, answering 25 percent of the questions, 75 percent of the questions, or another specified amount.

If using a computer to tabulate results, the evaluator should check for data entry errors, especially when the operator is entering the first responses. This will prevent recurring errors created when the operator misunderstands a task. If a staff is manually tabulating results, everybody should use the same tabulating system, and anyone tabulating results must understand the criteria for making decisions on questionable responses. Paraphrasing should be done carefully so as not to change the meaning of a response.

Three major tasks are involved in analyzing data: sorting the data, tabulating the data, and comparing raw data with summarized data. Regardless of the type of analysis used, analysis begins with sorting the data by respondent type, location, or some other identifying information. Sorting the data ensures that the information has been collected correctly.

Most inaccuracies in survey completion are caused by the respondent's misinterpretation of the directions. Sometimes interviews and observations cannot be completed because of some unforeseen problem at the time of the data collection; for example, the person being observed may be called away for an emergency or may experience extreme discomfort while being observed.

The goal of tabulation is to reduce data from its raw state into some type of quantified format without changing its meaning. Interpretation of the data cannot begin until it is tabulated and reduced. After condensing the raw data, the trainer can compare the two to ensure that the data has not been distorted.

When reporting information, certain parameters are followed, such as excluding the highest and lowest values if they are extremely outside the range, as well as excluding suspect data (with disclaimers). It is important to clearly state any known assumptions and bias, as well as any scale and labeling decisions.

For more information, see Module 4, *Measuring and Evaluating Training*, Chapter 5, "Interpretation and Reporting of Data."

# Appendix A
# Glossary

**ADDIE** is an instructional systems development model. It is composed of five phases:

- **Analysis** is the process of gathering data to identify specific needs: the who, what, where, when, and why of the design process.

- **Design** is the planning stage.

- **Development** is the phase in which training materials and content are selected and developed based on learning objectives.

- **Implementation** occurs when the course is delivered, whether in person or electronically.

- **Evaluation** is the ongoing process of developing and improving instructional materials based on evaluations conducted during and after implementation.

**Accelerated Learning** results in long-term retention by the learner. This is accomplished by honoring the different learning preferences of each individual learner and using experiential learning exercises (such as role plays, mnemonics, props, and music).

**Active Training** is an approach to training that ensures that participants are actively involved in the process. Active learning is based on the cooperative learning approach, in which participants learn from each other in pairs or small groups. Some examples of active training include group discussions, games, simulations, and role plays.

**Analysis** is the breaking up and examining of parts of a whole. In workplace learning and performance, these are some common analyses:

- **Gap analysis** identifies the discrepancy between the desired and actual knowledge, skills, and performance.

- **Root cause analysis** identifies the true cause(s) of the gap between desired and actual knowledge, skills, and performance.

- **Job analysis** identifies all duties and job responsibilities and the respective tasks done on a daily, weekly, monthly, or yearly basis that make up a single job function or role.

- **Needs analysis** is the process of collecting and synthesizing data to identify how training can help an organization reach its goals.

- **Task analysis** is the process of identifying the specific steps to correctly perform a task.

**Andragogy** (from the Greek meaning "adult learning"), is the adult learning theory popularized by Malcolm Knowles, based on five key principles that influence how adults learn: self-concept, prior experience, readiness to learn, orientation to learning, and motivation to learn.

**Asynchronous Training or Learning** refers to a scenario that does not require the trainer and the learner to participate at the same time or in the same location; email or threaded discussions are two examples.

**Behaviorism** is usually associated with psychologist and author B.F. Skinner and applies to psychology focused on observable and measurable behavioral change.

**Blended Learning** describes the practice of using several media in one curriculum. It typically refers to the combination of classroom instruction and any type of training that includes self-directed use of online capabilities.

**Bloom, Benjamin/Taxonomy of Learning** developed the three learning outcomes based on three domains: cognitive (knowledge), psychomotor (skills), and affective (attitude); sometimes referred to as KSAs.

**Brainstorming** is a group process for generating ideas in an uninhibited manner.

**Case study** is an example of a learning method in which a real or fictitious situation is presented for analysis and problem solving.

**Chunk** is a discrete portion of content, often consisting of several learning objects grouped together as a way to improve learner comprehension and retention. A trainer should break down and group, or chunk, larger pieces of information into smaller, easier-to-process groupings.

**Cognitivism** is the tell approach to learning, based on the theory that learning occurs through exposure to logically presented information, usually involving lecture. It can also include diagrams, videos, films, panels, class presentations, interviews with SMEs, readings, debates, and class studies.

**Competency-Based Learning** focuses on the learner, with heavy emphasis on individual learning plans. Features of competency-based learning are occupational analysis of competencies required for successful performance, validation of competencies, learner awareness of criteria and conditions for adequate or excellent performance, and planning for individual instruction and evaluation for each competency.

**Control group** is a group of participants in an experiment that is equal in all ways to the experimental group except for having received the experimental treatment (for example, a group of performers who have undergone training versus a group that has not).

**Criterion Reference** is an objective evaluation that focuses on assessing, analyzing, and reporting what learners have achieved based on the combination of performance standards and program objectives.

**Data Collection** refers to the collection of all facts, figures, statistics, and other information that are used for various types of analyses and assessments. Some examples of data-collection methods or tools are examinations of in-house or external written sources, questionnaires, interviews, and observation of trainees or jobholders.

**Delivery** is any method of transferring content to learners, including instructor-led training, WBT, CD-ROM, and books.

**Development** is learning or other types of activities that prepare a person for additional job responsibilities and enable him or her to gain knowledge or skills. It may also refer to the creation of training materials or courses. (See also *ADDIE.*)

**Distance Learning** is an educational situation in which the instructor and students are separated by time, location, or both. Education or training courses are delivered to remote locations via synchronous or asynchronous means of instruction.

**E-Learning** is a term covering a wide set of applications and processes, such as web-based learning, computer-based learning, virtual classrooms, and digital collaboration. Delivery of content may take place via the Internet, intranet/extranet (local area network [LAN]/wide area network [WAN]), audio- and videotape, satellite broadcast, interactive television, CD-ROM, and more.

**Electronic Performance Support System (EPSS)** is a computer application that's linked directly to another application to train or guide workers through completing a task in the target application. More generally, it is a computer or other device that gives workers information or resources to help them accomplish a task or achieve performance requirements. These systems deliver information on the job, just in time, and with minimum staff support.

**Enabling Objectives**, also called supporting objectives, support terminal objectives by breaking them down into more manageable chunks. Enabling objectives are the building blocks that provide additional concepts or skills needed to meet a terminal objective. (See also *Terminal Objectives.*)

**Evaluation** of training is a multilevel, systematic method for gathering information about the effectiveness and effect of training programs. Results of the measurements can be used to improve the offering, determine whether the learning objectives have been achieved, and assess the value of the training to the organization. Donald Kirkpatrick's four stages of evaluation, and Jack Phillips' fifth level of evaluation are:

- **Level 1: Reaction** evaluation focuses on the reaction of participants to the training program. Although this is the lowest level of measurement, it remains an important dimension to assess in terms of participant satisfaction.

- **Level 2: Learning** determines whether the participants actually learned what was intended for them to learn as a result of a training session. It measures the participant's acquisition of cognitive knowledge or behavioral skills.

- **Level 3: Behavior** focuses on the degree to which training participants are able to transfer their learning to their workplace behaviors.

- **Level 4: Results** is the last of Kirkpatrick's levels and moves beyond the training participant to assess the effect of the learning on organizational performance.

- **Level 5: Return-on-Investment (ROI)** is a higher level of evaluation that compares the monetary benefits of training programs with program costs, usually presented as a percentage or benefit-and-cost ratio. Level 5 evaluation is not part of the Kirkpatrick model, but was developed by Jack Phillips.

**Experience-Centered** is a cognitivism-based theory of instruction focused on the learner's experience during instruction and production of fresh insights.

**Experiential Learning Activities (ELAs)** are ways of learning that stress experience and reflection and use an inductive learning process that takes the learner through five stages: experiencing, publishing, processing, generalizing, and applying.

**Extant Data** comprises existing records, reports, and data that may be available inside or outside the organization. Examples include job descriptions, competency models, benchmarking reports, annual reports, financial statements, strategic plans, mission statements, staffing statistics, climate surveys, 360-degree feedback, performance appraisals, grievances, turnover rates, absenteeism, suggestion box feedback, accident statistics, and so forth.

**Facilitation** refers to the role of the person or trainer who guides or makes learning easier, both in content and in application of the content to the job.

**Feedback** is advice or information given from one person to another about how useful or successful an event, process, or action is. Feedback is given to participants after training regarding their progress, which helps with retention and behavior.

**Functional Context** describes training that relates to actual job circumstances because training is successful only when learners can carry out learned tasks at their actual workstations. For example, a learner may be able to diagnose a mechanical problem and perform a series of repair steps in a logical, timely way during the training course. But if actual work conditions are noisy and chaotic, those conditions may need to be simulated during training. (See also *Competency-Based Learning*.)

**Gagne, Robert/Conditions of Learning** was a pioneer in the field of instructional design. He is best known for popularizing the theory of nine instructional events that help ensure learning occurs:

1. Gain the learners' attention.
2. Share the objectives of the session.
3. Ask learners to recall prior learning.
4. Deliver content.
5. Use methods to enhance understanding (for example, case studies or graphs).
6. Provide an opportunity to practice.
7. Provide feedback.
8. Assess performance.
9. Provide job aids or references to ensure transfer to the job.

**Gardner, Howard** designed multiple intelligence theory, an accelerated learning theory that states there is no single way in which everyone thinks and learns. Gardner devised a list of eight intelligences: verbal-linguistic, logical-mathematical, visual-spatial, bodily-kinesthetic, musical-rhythmic, interpersonal, intrapersonal, and naturalistic, which, in different combinations, make up a person's learning style.

**Goal** refers to an end state or condition toward which human effort is directed.

**Herrmann Brain Dominance Instrument** is a method of personality testing developed by W.E. (Ned) Herrmann that classifies learners in terms of preferences for thinking in the four different modes based on brain function: left brain, cerebral; left brain, limbic; right brain, limbic; right brain, cerebral. (See also *Learning Style).*

**Human Performance Improvement (HPI)** is a results-based, systematic process used to identify performance problems, analyze root causes, select and design actions, manage learning in the workplace, measure results, and continuously improve performance within an organization. It is based on open systems theory, or the view that any organization in a system that absorbs environmental inputs, uses them in transformational processes, and expels them as outputs.

**Human Performance Technology (HPT)** is a systems view of human performance that is used to analyze both a performance gap and a performance system. It is necessary to select and design cost-effective and efficient learning programs that are strategically aligned to support organization goals and values. It is sometimes interchanged with HPI.

**Icebreakers** are activities conducted at the beginning of training programs that introduce participants to one another; may introduce content; and in general, help participants ease into the program.

**Interview Protocol** is a page with interview questions already printed on it with room for notes. The interviewer uses the interview protocol to make notes for each question.

**ISD (Instructional Systems Development)** is a systems approach to analyzing, designing, developing, implementing, and evaluating any instructional experience based on the belief that training is most effective when it provides learners with a clear statement of what they must be able to do as a result of training and how their performance will be evaluated.

**Instructional Strategies**, sometimes called presentation strategies, are the mechanisms through which instruction is presented.

**Job Aids** provide guidance or assistance, either audio or visual, to the performer about when to carry out tasks and steps, thereby reducing the amount of recall necessary and minimizing error. Usually tasks that are performed with relatively low frequency, that are highly complex, that are likely to change in the future, or have a high probability of error are good candidates for job aids.

**Job Analysis** identifies all duties and responsibilities and the respective tasks performed on a daily, weekly, monthly, or yearly basis that make up a single job function or role (See also *Analysis.*)

**Just-in-Time Training** provides learning when it is actually needed and used on the job.

**Kirkpatrick, Donald** is considered the father of training evaluation, which he first postulated in the 1950s. He created the four levels of evaluation: reaction, learning, behavior, and results. (See also *Evaluation*.)

**Knowles, Malcolm**, considered the father of adult learning theory, Knowles defined a set of assumptions about adult learning and published *The Adult Learner: A Neglected Species*, in 1973.

**KSA** is an abbreviation with two definitions: **1.** Knowledge (or cognitive), skills (or psychomotor), and *attitude* (or affective) are the three objective domains of learning defined by Benjamin Bloom's taxonomy in the 1950s. **2.** Knowledge, skills, and *ability* are commonly referred to as KSAs and are used by federal and private hiring agencies to determine the attributes or qualities that an employee possesses for a particular job.

**Learning** is the process of gaining knowledge, understanding, or skill by study, instruction, or experience.

**Learning Style** describes an individual's approach to learning that involves the way he or she behaves, feels, and processes information. (See also *Herrmann Brain Dominance Instrument;* and *VAK Model*.)

**Likert Scale** is a linear scale used in data collection to rate statements and attitudes; for example, respondents receive a definition of the scale from 1 to 10.

**Mager, Robert** developed behavioral learning objectives with three elements: what the worker must do (performance), the conditions under which the work must be done, and the standard or criterion that is considered acceptable performance.

**Maslow's Hierarchy of Needs** refers to Abraham Maslow and was introduced in 1954 in his book *Motivation and Personality*. Maslow contended that people have complex needs that they strive to fulfill, and that change and evolve over time. He categorized these needs as physiological, safety/security, social/belongingness, esteem, and self-actualization, with the basic needs having to be satisfied before an individual can focus on growth.

**Modules** (sometimes called lessons) are the smallest unit of learning and provide content and practice on the basis of predefined learning objectives. Learning modules contain objectives, knowledge content to enable the learner to complete the task, task content, practice activities to help reach the objective or objectives, and an assessment mechanism to determine whether the objectives were reached.

**Multiple Intelligence Theory**, popularized by Howard Gardner in *Frames of Mind* (1985), describes how intelligences reflect how people prefer to process information. Gardner believes that most people are comfortable in three to four of these intelligences and avoid the others. For example, for learners who are not comfortable working with others, doing group case studies may interfere with their ability to process new material.

**Neurolinguistic Programming** is a style of communication and behavior change management that is based on observations and analyses of unconscious physical behaviors that identify patterns of feeling or thought.

**Objective** is a target or purpose that, when combined with other objectives, leads to a goal. The following are some examples of particular types of learning-related objectives:

- **Behavioral objectives** specify the particular new behavior that an individual should be able to perform after training.

- **Affective objectives** are learning objectives that specify the acquisition of particular attitudes, values, or feelings.

- **Learning objectives** are clear, measurable, statements of behavior that a learner demonstrates when the training is considered a success.

**Objective-Centered** is a behaviorism-based theory of instruction that concentrates on observable and measurable outcomes.

**Opportunity-Centered** is a developmentalism-based theory of instruction that focuses on matching individual needs to appropriate instructional experiences. Opportunity-centered instruction is particularly useful for helping employees adapt to changes in their work lives.

**Pedagogy** is an informal philosophy of teaching that focuses on what the instructor does rather than what the participants learn. Usually refers to the teaching of children.

**Phillips, Jack** is a well-known evaluation expert who has developed a fifth level of evaluation, ROI, in training programs. (See also *Evaluation, Level5: ROI*).

**Project Management** is the planning, organizing, directing, and controlling of resources for a finite period of time to complete specific goals and objectives.

**RID (Rapid Instructional Design)** is a collection of strategies for quickly producing instructional packages to enable a group of learners to achieve a set of specific instructional objectives.

**Role Play** is an activity in which participants act out roles, attitudes, or behaviors that are not their own to practice skills or apply what they have learned. Frequently an observer provides feedback to those in character.

**SDL (Self-Directed Learning)** is individualized, or self-paced learning that generally refers to programs that use a variety of delivery media, ranging from print products to web-based systems. It can also refer to less formal types of learning, such as team learning, knowledge management systems, and self-development programs.

**SME (Subject Matter Expert)** is a person who has extensive knowledge and skills in a particular subject area.

**Subjective-centered** is a pedagogy-based instructional approach. Subject-centered instruction focuses on what will be taught as opposed to learner-related characteristics. Subject-centered instruction focuses on learner acquisition of information.

**Synchronous Training** refers to a scenario that involves the trainer and the trainee participating at the same time. It often refers to e-learning or WBT.

**Terminal Objectives** are the final behavioral outcomes of a specific instructional event. The designer must state an objective clearly and describe the intended exit competencies for the specified unit, lesson, course, or program for which it was written.

**Trainer** is a person who helps individuals improve performance by teaching, instructing, or facilitating learning in an organization.

**Training Objective** is a statement of what the instructor hopes to accomplish during the training session.

**VAK Model** is a model of the way that individuals learn and retain information. Some people learn primarily through one learning style, others through a combination of the three: visual (learners need pictures, diagrams, and other visuals), audio (learners need to hear information), and kinesthetic (learners need hands-on learning).

**Virtual Classroom** is an online learning space where learners and instructors interact.

WBT (Web-Based Training) is delivery of educational content via a web browser over the public Internet, a private intranet, or an extranet.

**WLP (Workplace Learning and Performance)** refers to the professions of training, performance improvement, learning, development, and workplace education. It often is colloquially referred to as training or training and development.

# Appendix B
# Answer Key

## Chapter 1

**1.** A WLP professional is tailoring instructional materials to the leadership training needs of her executives. This is an example of

A. The application of adult learning theory in designing instruction

*Response A is correct because tailoring instructional materials to executive leadership training needs is an example of ensuring that the design of materials relates to the different ways that adults learn, which is one method to apply adult learning theory.*

**2.** When a WLP professional focuses identifying observable and measurable outcomes for his training on ethics and business conduct, which theory of learning and instruction is being applied?

B. Objective-centered

*Response B, objective-centered learning, is correct because it is a behaviorism-centered theory of instruction that concentrates on observable and measurable outcomes.*

**3.** Which of the following best describes why Maslow's hierarchy of needs is important in relation to adult learning?

D. Five levels of needs indicate that a person only can achieve a higher level of need after lower levels are satisfied, which suggests people are motivated by different factors—factors that may be unknown or difficult to discern.

*Response D is correct because Maslow's hierarchy of needs categorizes five levels of needs—starting with the most basic: physiological, safety, belongingness, esteem, and self-actualization—that people fulfill at different times, which means that people are motivated by different things.*

**4.** In the field of workplace learning and performance, what is Malcolm Knowles's key contribution to adult learning?

A. Andragogy

*Response A is correct because Malcolm Knowles was one of the first researchers to propose that adults learn differently from children. To indicate the differences, Knowles popularized the terms andragogy and pedagogy.*

**5.** Which of the following is not an adult learning characteristic based on the andragogy model?

C. As people mature, their readiness to learn is directly related to age level and curriculum.

*Response C is correct because age level and curriculum are not two of the five key principles of andragogy.*

**6.** Adult development theories are concerned with

A. How adults change as they age and the effect on learning

*Response A is correct because adult development theories relate to how adults change as they age, focusing on how the broad themes of learning and development are intertwined from three major perspectives: physical, psychological, and socio-cultural.*

**7.** A new sales training program focused on improving the motivation of the sales force is most likely to focus on which of the following Bloom categories of learning?

C. Attitude

*Response C is correct because attitude is one of three types of learning—knowledge, skills, and attitude, typically referred to as KSAs—that are part of Benjamin Bloom's taxonomy of learning and refers to how people deal with things emotionally, such as feelings, motivation, and enthusiasm.*

**8.** Which of the following guidelines did Carl Rogers describe as a critical element to remember in adult learning situations?

D. Facilitators establish the initial mood or climate of the class experience and clarify the purpose of the individuals in the class as well as more general purposes of the group.

*Response D is correct because Carl Rogers proposed several theories of personality and behavior and applied them to education. This process led him to the concept of learner-centered teaching. Establishing the initial mood or climate of the class experience and clarifying the purpose of the individuals in the class as well as more general purposes of the group are two of eight guidelines based on Rogers's work that help to facilitate learning.*

**9.** Which of the following theories of learning focuses on matching individual needs to appropriate instructional experiences and is particularly useful for helping employees adapt to changes in their work lives?

D. Opportunity-centered

*Response D is correct because opportunity-centered learning is a developmentalism-based theory of instruction that focuses on matching individual needs with appropriate instructional experiences.*

**10.** Cognitivism is an approach based on the principle that

C. Learning occurs primarily through exposure to logically presented information and is interested in the organization of memory and thinking.

*Response C is correct because cognitivism concerns itself with the organization of memory and thinking based on a model of the mind as an information-processing system.*

**11.** Which learning theory seeks to involve the right and left hemispheres of the brain and the cortex and the limbic systems of the brain in learning—and by involving the different functions makes learning more natural?

B. Accelerated learning

*Response B is correct because accelerated learning is a method of learning that involves all systems of the brain and thereby makes learning more natural. Principles involved in accelerated learning are affective state, beliefs toward learning, information networks, nonconscious learning, learning cycles, multisensory input, and learning readiness state.*

**12.** According to the VAK model, when designing learning for kinesthetic learners, which of the following should be included based on their preferred mode of learning?

C. Hands-on activities

*Response C is correct because hands-on activities are an example of intake by doing and touching, which is the kinesthetic preference out of the three types of learner preferences categorized by the VAK model.*

**13.** Which of the following theories and models is associated with Howard Gardner?

A. Multiple intelligences

*Response A is correct because Howard Gardner suggested that intelligence is more multifaceted than previously thought and that traditional intelligence measures are not capable of measuring all its facets.*

# Chapter 2

1. What does ADDIE stand for?

C. Analyze, design, develop, implement, evaluate

*Response C is correct because the ADDIE model, which stands for analysis, design, development, implementation, and evaluation, is one of the most fundamental instructional systems development models, which provides instructional designers with the necessary structure to design any curriculum.*

**2.** Which of the following best describes the key benefit of Gagne's nine instructional events?

B. This theory supports the notion of lesson plan design and an ideal teaching sequence that enhances retention because training is based on the way that learners process information.

*Response B is correct because Gagne built the nine events of instruction based on the work of other theorists who studied the way humans process information and move it from sensing to processing to storing it in short- or long-term memory.*

**3.** Which of the following instructional design models is based on the assumption that design happens in a context of project management where a project plan establishes roles, tasks, timelines, budgets, checkpoints, and supervisory procedures?

C. Seels and Glasgow instructional systems design model

*Response C is correct because Barbara Seels and Rita Glasgow presented an instructional systems design model that assumes design takes place within the context of project management.*

**4.** Which of the following instructional design models states that a designer goes through a three-stage process: analysis, strategy development, and evaluation?

D. Smith and Ragan systematic instructional design model

*Response D is correct because Smith and Ragan believe that analysis, strategy development, and evaluation are the stages common to most instructional design models. Their model also differs from most instructional design models in that test items are written within the analysis stage right after tasks are analyzed.*

**5.** Accelerated learning is a learning strategy that involves both the right and left hemispheres and the cortex and limbic systems of the brain, thus making learning more natural. Which of the following is *not* a characteristic of a learning environment that is conducive to accelerated learning?

A. Provides learning challenges for learners to overcome

*Response A is correct because an accelerated learning environment does not provide learning challenges for learners to overcome.*

**6.** Sequencing of instruction is important to its effectiveness. Which of the following is *not* a type of sequencing?

D. Performance/skill

*Response D is correct because performance/skill is not a type of sequence. Instruction is usually sequenced in order of priority or frequency.*

**7.** A client wants a designer to develop a training class to improve declining sales of the salesforce. What is the best thing to do first?

B. Perform a front-end analysis

*Response B is correct because the information training sponsors provide about the audience, the material that a course needs to cover, and the completion date may not address the organization's specific training requirements. When starting a learning project, the instructional designer's first task is to identify those requirements through a front-end analysis.*

**8.** Which of the following is a principle of human performance improvement?

B. Training may not be the appropriate solution, and a needs analysis should be conducted to ensure that the performance gap can be remedied by training.

*Response B is correct because taking a training class alone does not always result in measurable changes in workplace behavior. This happens because training addresses only one driver of performance: skills and knowledge. In instances where workers do have the skills and knowledge to handle*

*a task but still do not perform it effectively, another factor may affect performance. A needs analysis will enable the workplace learning and performance (WLP) professional to determine if training is an appropriate solution.*

**9.** Who is credited with the idea that a learning objective should contain a condition statement, a performance statement, and a criterion statement?

D. Robert Mager

*Response D is correct because Robert Mager argued for the use of specific, measurable objectives that both guide designers during courseware development and aid participants in the learning process. These behavioral, performance, or criteria-referenced objectives should contain a condition statement, a performance statement, and a criterion statement.*

**10.** Which of the following is described as a collection of strategies for quickly producing instructional packages that enable learners to achieve a set of specific learning objectives? This model involves alternatives, enhancements, and modifications to the ADDIE model in the form of tradeoffs between design and delivery.

A. Rapid instructional design

*Response A is correct because in rapid instructional design, the selection of appropriate instructional development techniques depends on trading off resources between design and delivery of instruction depending on the nature of the instructional objective, characteristics of the learner, and context of training.*

**11.** Which of the following best describes Bloom's taxonomy and its relevance to writing objectives?

C. Because learning objectives are written to specify the performance (knowledge and skill) that is desired after the learning, the taxonomy specifies exactly what the learner will know or be able to do at the end of the training experience.

*Response C is correct because Benjamin Bloom identified the cognitive, psychomotor, and affective learning domains (later expanded), which relate to the terms used to describe three categories of learning: knowledge, skills, and attitude. These in turn relate to writing objectives because learning objectives specify the type of performance that is expected after the training (knowledge or skills), for example, "will be able to apply" not just "name."*

**12.** Which of the following objective domains—categories of objectives used to determine design elements—focuses on the skills and knowledge relating to intellectual activity, such as knowing how to edit a manuscript?

A. Cognitive

*Response A is correct because the cognitive objective domain refers to skills and knowledge related to intellectual activity.*

**13.** Instruction on how to operate a forklift is most likely to have which type of objective?

B. Psychomotor

*Response B is correct because operating a forklift relates to physical activity and is thus most likely to be a psychomotor objective.*

# Chapter 3

**1.** The instructional design of a virtual live session on handling difficult customers for a call center is primarily based on which of the following inputs?

A. Needs assessment of training requirements and learning objectives

*Response A is correct because designing e-learning uses the same ADDIE model and tools as designing any other instruction, thus the virtual live session will be primarily based on a needs assessment and learning objectives just as designing any other instruction would be.*

**2.** An in-depth analysis of the characteristics of potential learners for a change management course will most likely *not* include investigation of which of the following?

D. Media

*Response D is correct because media is not included in an analysis of learner characteristics.*

3. Using games as a part of instruction is most beneficial to what type of learner?

C. Adults who gather information actively

*Response C is correct because using games is a way to get learners involved in gathering information actively. Other techniques that appeal to adults who prefer to gather information actively are group*

*discussions, readings, simulations or role-plays, programmed instruction, and case studies.*

**4.** Which of the following best describes simulations?

A. An exercise that includes a form of real-life situation so participants can practice making decisions and analyze the results of those decisions.

*Response A is correct because simulations duplicate the essential features of a task and enable people to practice the task to master skills and gain understanding. Simulation exposes learners to a broad array of scenarios in a short period of time, allowing them to see the results of decisions play out quickly, so that they can relate to outcomes more easily.*

**5.** Which type of feedback should be designed into an e-learning course in which learners are learning customer service skills?

B. Intrinsic

*Response B is correct because intrinsic feedback allows learners to see for themselves if their performance works as well as it needs to by showing the consequences of their errors. In learning customer service skills, intrinsic feedback is more effective because it allows learners to adjust their behavior and continue to refine their understanding of the topic as they learn.*

# Chapter 6

**1.** Which of the following is *not* one of the basic roles of a designer on a project?

A. The designer has little if any content knowledge and relies on the SME to select the most appropriate instructional strategy and media.

*Response A is not one of the basic roles of designers because the designer always selects the most appropriate instructional strategy and media.*

**2.** The primary role of an SME on a project includes all of the following *except*

C. Establishes the goals of the instruction and supplies the content

*Response C is correct because the SME does not establish the goals of the instruction; that is part of the role of the designer.*

**3.** Which of the following is *not* one of the techniques used by designers when working with SMEs to uncover and to distinguish what needs to be included in the instruction?

C. Evaluation techniques

*Response C is correct because designers use evaluation techniques to evaluate the effectiveness of the learning solution, not to uncover and distinguish what needs to be included in the instruction.*

# Chapter 7

1. Which of the following best describes training needs assessment, which is often also referred to as training needs analysis?

A. Training needs assessment is the process of collecting and synthesizing data to identify training requirements.

*Response A is correct because the classical approach to determining training requirements is by gathering data through interviews, observations, questionnaires, and tests.*

2. All of the following are benefits of conducting a needs assessment *except*

C. Training managers to train content to their department personnel

*Response C is correct because training managers to train their personnel is not a benefit of a needs assessment.*

3. All of the following are steps in conducting a training needs assessment *except*

C. Selecting learning strategies

*Response C is correct because selecting learning strategies is part of the design component of developing instruction.*

4. Which of the following is one way that an organization can find out what kind of training and development should be promoted?

A. Conduct a needs assessment.

*Response A is correct because a training needs assessment places the training requirement in the context of the organization's needs and validates and augments the initial issues presented by sponsor of the training.*

5. Which of the following is an advantage of using interviews as a data-gathering technique?

A. Interviewers can receive additional information in the form of nonverbal messages. Interviewees' behaviors—their gestures, eye contact, and general reactions to questions—are additional data or cues for the next questions.

*Response A is correct because interviews, or one-on-one discussions, elicit the reactions of interviewees to carefully focused topics. This data-collection method yields subjective and perceptive individual data and illustrative anecdotes. Because they enable the interviewer to observe the reactions of the interviewee, the interviewer gets additional information to pursue. Interviews have other advantages, including providing rich detail, enabling comparisons across interviews when a carefully structured protocol is used, and supplementing quantitative data gathered from surveys.*

6. Which of the following instruments has participants rate two contrasting ideas or words that are separated by a graduated line, either numbered or unnumbered? They indicate frequency of behavior or depth of opinion by circling points on the line.

B. Semantic differential

*Response B is correct because in a survey that uses a semantic differential, participants rate two contrasting ideas or words separated by a graduated line, either numbered or unnumbered.*

7. Designers should rely primarily on one data-gathering technique to ensure consistency and accuracy of results.

B. False

*The statement is false because designers should use multiple data-gathering techniques because several sources of data are more likely to produce accurate needs assessments than one and because designers are better able to validate their data.*

8. Which of the following is used to identify the efficiency and effectiveness of employees?

A. Performance audit

*Response A is correct because learning professionals use performance audits to identify the efficiency and effectiveness of employees by comparing clear performance criteria with actual performance data.*

**9.** Quantitative methods of collecting data are those that result in

C. Hard data

*Response C is correct because hard data is objective and measurable, whether stated in terms of frequency, percentage, proportion, or time.*

# Chapter 14

**1.** Which of the following is an advantage of asynchronous web-based training?

C. Greater flexibility for participants

*Response C is correct because asynchronous web-based training refers to a learning environment in which the trainer and learners do not have to participate at the same time, which allows the learner to participate in the training at a time that is most convenient for him or her.*

**2.** Which of the following is a disadvantage of asynchronous web-based training?

A. Requires excellent instructional design and production

*Response A is correct because the training must have excellent design and production to keep learners engaged with asynchronous web-based training, which requires more time, money, and other resources.*

3. A WLP professional has decided to design an asynchronous web-based program to provide ongoing performance support among the field sales staff. Is the selection of asynchronous web-based training appropriate and why?

A. Yes, because this training approach will allow learners to access the training as needed

*Response A is correct because the trainer and learners do not have to participate at the same time in asynchronous web-based training, which enables field sales staff to access training and ongoing performance support on demand.*

**4.** A WLP professional has decided to design a class to provide ongoing performance support among the field sales staff. Is the selection of classroom training appropriate and why?

D. No, because this training approach often causes training and performance support to be approached as separate efforts

*Response D is correct because asynchronous web-based training facilitates seamless connection between training and performance support whereas classroom training is limited to a time and a place and is thus more detached from performance support.*

**5.** Which of the following is an advantage of classroom learning?

A. Some learners may be more comfortable with classroom training because they may be more familiar with a traditional training environment.

*Response A is correct because classroom training is the most familiar training environment for many people. An increased comfort level can enable learners to be most receptive to the learning.*

# Appendix C
# Index

in design phase, 51–52
domains of, 47–48
enabling, 46
evaluation and, 42
in Gagne's nine events of
   instruction, 35–37
goals vs., 43–44
hierarchy of, 45
implementation of, 34
instructional strategies
   and, 51–52
knowledge, skills, and
   attitudes (KSAs), 40
Mager's behavioral, 44–45
motivation and, 11
terminal, 45–46
theories, learning and
   instruction, 2
observations, 117–18
organizations
   assessment of, 110
   culture of, 12–13
   drivers, 133–34
   strategies, 133
outcomes of key actions,
   vi–vii
outputs
   development of, 66
   of learning designers, vii

**P**

pedagogy, 4–5
performance audits, 115
presentation methods, 91
presentation strategies. *See*
   instructional strategies
programmed learning, 13
psychomotor, 9, 46–47, 60,
   74

**Q**

questions
   for data collection, 113
   for e-learning, 144–45

**R**

rapid instructional design
   (RID), 37
reports, design, 56
research, evaluation, 135–36
resources, 64
results, measurable, 28–30
Rogers, Carl, 10
role plays, 81

**S**

Seels and Glasgow ISD
   Model II, 38–39
simulations, 81–83
Smith and Ragan Systematic
   Instructional Design model,
   39, 41
software, collaborative
   learning, 130
strengths, weaknesses,
   opportunities, and threats
   (SWOT) analysis, 134
subject matter experts
   (SMEs), 95–99
surveys, 120–23

**T**

task analysis, 51, 94, 111–12
task assessments, 111–12
taxonomy, Bloom's, 9, 46–47
teaching, facilitation vs., 9–10
techniques
   active training, 79–81
   e-learning, 81–82
   grading content, 59–60,
      65–66
tests, 114–15
theories
   adult development, 6–9
   adult learning, vi–viii, 1–2
   behaviorism, 2, 11, 13–14
   cognition and adult
      learning, vi–vii, 1–2
   cognitivism, 14
time, 57–58, 85

tips, data collection, 124–25
trainings, 79–81, 99
   *See also specific types*

**V**

visual, auditory, and kinestic
   (VAK) model, 17–18

**W**

web-based training (WBT),
   84–87, 141–43, 147
   *See also* computer-based
      training (CBT); e-
      learning
work samples, 123